Japan Faces the World, 1925–1952

We work with leading authors to develop the
strongest educational materials in history,
bringing cutting-edge thinking and best learning
practice to a global market.

Under a range of well-known imprints, including
Longman, we craft high-quality print and electronic
publications which help readers to understand and
apply their content, whether studying or at work.

To find out more about the complete range of our
publishing please visit us on the World Wide Web at:
www.pearsoneduc.com

SEMINAR STUDIES   IN HISTORY

Japan Faces the World
1925–1952

MARY L. HANNEMAN

An imprint of **Pearson Education**

Harlow, England · London · New York · Reading, Massachusetts · San Francisco · Toronto · Don Mills, Ontario · Sydney
Tokyo · Singapore · Hong Kong · Seoul · Taipei · Cape Town · Madrid · Mexico City · Amsterdam · Munich · Paris · Milan

Pearson Education Limited
Edinburgh Gate
Harlow
Essex CM20 2JE
England
and Associated Companies throughout the world.

Visit us on the World Wide Web at:
www.pearsoneduc.com

First published 2001

ISBN 0-582-36898-7

British Library Cataloguing-in-Publication Data
A catalogue record for this book is
available from the British Library

Library of Congress Cataloging-in-Publication Data
Hanneman, Mary
    Japan faces the world, 1925–1952 / Mary Hanneman.
        p. cm. -- (Seminar studies in history)
    Includes bibliographical references and index.
    ISBN 0-582-36898-7 (limp : alk. paper)
        1. Japan--History--1926–1945. 2. Japan--History--Allied occupation, 1945–1952.
    3. Japan--History--1912–1926. 4. Sino-Japanese Conflict, 1937–1945. 5. World War,
    1939–1945. 6. World politics--20th century. I. Title. II. Series.

    DS888.5 . H2426 2001
    952.03'3--dc21   2001029316

10 9 8 7 6 5 4 3 2 1
05 04 03 02 01 00

Set by 7 in 10/12 Sabon Roman
Printed in Malaysia , LSP

CONTENTS

INTRODUCTION TO THE SERIES

Such is the pace of historical enquiry in the modern world that there is an ever-widening gap between the specialist article or monograph, incorporating the results of current research, and general surveys, which inevitably become out of date. *Seminar Studies in History* is designed to bridge this gap. The series was founded by Patrick Richardson in 1966 and his aim was to cover major themes in British, European and world history. Between 1980 and 1996 Roger Lockyer continued his work, before handing the editorship over to Clive Emsley and Gordon Martel. Clive Emsley is Professor of History at the Open University, while Gordon Martel is Professor of International History at the University of Northern British Columbia, Canada, and Senior Research Fellow at De Montfort University.

All the books are written by experts in their field who are not only familiar with the latest research but have often contributed to it. They are frequently revised, in order to take account of new information and interpretations. They provide a selection of documents to illustrate major themes and provoke discussion, and also a guide to further reading. The aim of *Seminar Studies in History* is to clarify complex issues without over-simplifying them, and to stimulate readers into deepening their knowledge and understanding of major themes and topics.

AUTHOR'S ACKNOWLEDGEMENTS

Working on this book has been an enjoyable process. I would like to thank Gordon Matel for asking me to produce this book for the series. Sarah Bury has been invaluable in gently guiding the project through to its completion. Copy-editor Jane Raistrick's keen attention to detail enabled us to eliminate a number of problems before publication. John Nelson, at the University of Washington, Tacoma, scanned all the documents for me. I thank them all for their kind assistance.

I would also like to thank my parents, Donna S. Hanneman and Carl F. Hanneman. My mother happily took care of the kids on numerous occasions while I wrote; my father's early career in Tokyo started my interest in Japan.

My children, Jim, Davy and Caroline Allen, are a constant joy to me and help make it all worthwhile. Finally, many thanks to my husband, Michael Allen, for his tireless support and devotion.

PUBLISHER'S ACKNOWLEDGEMENTS

We are indebted to the following for permission to reproduce copyright material:

Stanford University Press for an extract translated in *Japan's Decision for War: Records of the 1941 Policy Conferences*, edited by Ike Nobutaka (Stanford, CA, 1967) pp. 135–49 and an extract by Emperor Hirohito translated in *Japan's Decision to Surrender*, by Robert J.C. Bulow (Stanford, CA, 1954).

We have been unable to trace the copyright holder of William Theodore de Bary, *Sources of Japanese Tradition*, by William Theodore de Bary (New York, 1958) and would appreciate any information which would enable us to do so.

CHRONOLOGY

1868

3 January   Meiji Restoration.

1890

11 February   Promulgation of the Meiji Constitution.

30 October   Imperial Rescript on Education.

1894

July   Japan attacks China; Sino-Japanese War begins.

1895

17 April   Japan gains Taiwan in Treaty of Shimonoseki, which ends the Sino-Japanese War.

1904

8 February   Japan attacks Russia; Russo-Japanese War begins.

1905

5 September   Treaty of Portsmouth ends Russo-Japanese War; Japan establishes a Protectorate over Korea.

1910

22 July   Japan annexes Korea.

1912

30 July   Death of the Meiji Emperor; commencement of the Taisho reign period with accession of son, Yoshihito.

1914

23 August   Japan declares war on Germany.

1915

18 January   Japan issues Twenty-One Demands to China; growing anti-Japanese sentiment in China.

1918

August   Rice Riots.

1921

November   Hirohito becomes regent to his father.

November   Assassination attempt on Regent Hirohito.

1923

1 September   Kanto Earthquake.

1924

                    Japanese Exclusion Act enacted by US Congress.

1925

March   Peace Preservation Law and Universal Manhood Suffrage
                    Law enacted.

1926

25 December   Death of Taisho Emperor; commencement of Showa reign
                    period.

1927

July   Japanese troops to China in the Shandong Expedition.

                    Prime Minister Tanaka Giichi announces 'Positive Policy'
                    toward China.

1928

20 February   First general election with universal male suffrage.

15 March   Police round-up of radicals and leftists under Peace
                    Preservation Law.

4 June   Assassination of Manchurian warlord Zhang Zuolin.

1930

22 April   London Naval Treaty.

14 November   Prime Minister Hamaguchi assassination attempt.

1931

18 September   Manchurian Incident.

1932

1 March   Establishment of Japanese puppet state of Manchukuo.

15 May   Assassination of government leaders in Showa Restoration
                    attempt.

26 May   Prime Minister Saito appoints 'cabinet of national unity'.

1933

24 February   Adoption of Lytton Report by League of Nations.

Summer   Repudiations of communist belief by Nabeyama Sadachika
                    and Sano Manabu.

1935

Public denunciations of Minobe Tatsukichi for emperor organ theory.

1936

26 February   Army First Division cordons off downtown Tokyo in Showa Restoration attempt.

25 November   Anti-Comintern Pact between Japan and Germany.

December   Xian Incident in China leads to creation of anti-Japanese united front between Chinese Nationalists and Communists.

1937

March   Publication of *Kokutai no hongi*.

7 July   China Incident, clash of Japanese and Chinese troops near Beijing, leads to outbreak of war with China.

December   Rape of Nanjing.

1938

Summer   US embargoes war *matériel* to Japan.

11 November   Prime Minister Konoe announces 'New Order in East Asia'.

1939

1 September   Outbreak of war in Europe.

1940

March   Wang Jingwei establishes Japanese puppet regime in Nanjing.

23 September   Japanese troops to Indochina.

27 September   Tripartite Pact with Germany and Italy.

12 October   Imperial Rule Assistance Association established.

1941

8 March   Negotiations begin between Ambassador Nomura and Secretary of State Hull.

13 April   Japan–Soviet Neutrality Pact.

21 June   Hitler invades Soviet Union.

24 July   Japanese troops occupy Indochina.

26 July   US embargoes oil sales and shipments to Japan.

6 September   Imperial Conference adopts decision to wage war with the US while continuing to pursue negotiations.

18 October   General Tojo Hideki becomes Prime Minister.

26 November   'Hull Note' reiterates US demands for return to *status quo ante* 1931.

7 December   Japan attacks Pearl Harbor.

| December–May 1942 | Japan gains control over Singapore, Guam, Wake Island, Hong Kong, Malaya, Dutch East Indies, Philippine Islands, and Burma. |

1942

| 3-5 June | Battle of Midway. |

1943

February	Japan driven from Guadalcanal.
April	Admiral Yamamoto Isoroku shot down over Solomon Islands.
November	Gilbert Islands under Allied control.

1944

March	Marshall Islands under Allied control.
19 June – 9 July	Saipan falls to US control.
24 November	B-29 bombing campaigns on Japan begin.
22 July	Tojo resigns premiership.
20–24 October	Battle of Leyte Gulf.

1945

4 March	Luzon under Allied control.
5 February	Philippines under Allied control.
February	Iwo Jima under Allied control.
1 April–23 June	Battle of Okinawa.
8 May	German surrender.
26 July	Potsdam Declaration.
6 August	Atomic bomb on Hiroshima.
8 August	Soviets enter war against Japan.
9 August	Atomic bomb on Nagasaki.
14 August	Japanese surrender; acceptance of terms of Potsdam Declaration.
28 August	Allied troops arrive in Japan; Occupation begins.
2 September	Formal surrender signed on USS *Missouri*.

1946

1 January	Emperor Hirohito renounces his divinity.
3 May	War crimes trials open.
October	Land Reform Law enacted.

1947

| 1 February | Prime Minister Yoshida prohibits general strike; first indications of the 'Reverse Course'. |
| 3 May | Postwar Constitution in effect. |

1948

23 December   Execution of Class 'A' war criminals, including Tojo.

1950

25 June   North Korea invades South Korea.

10 August   Creation of National Police Reserve.

1951

11 April   General MacArthur dismissed; replaced by Matthew Ridgeway.

8 September   San Francisco Peace Treaty signed.

8 September   US–Japan Mutual Security Treaty signed.

1952

28 April   Peace treaty in effect, ending Occupation.

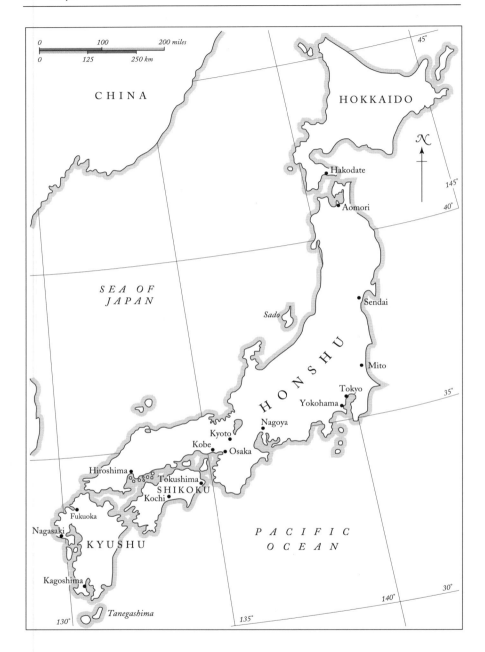

Map 1 Japan, 1925

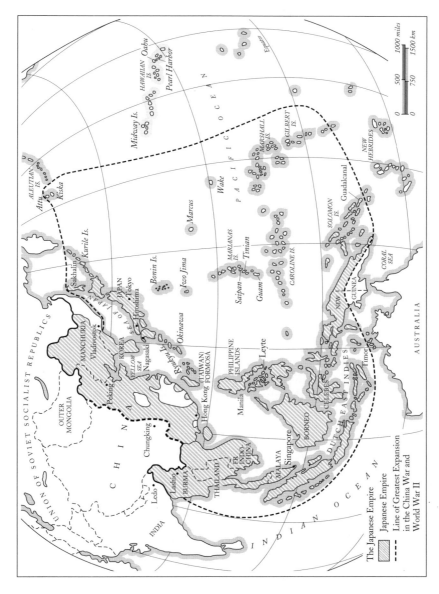

Map 2   The largest extent of the Japanese Empire, early 1942

PART ONE INTRODUCTION

CHAPTER ONE

BACKGROUND AND HISTORIOGRAPHY

In 1868, a group of young samurai banded together to overthrow the moribund Tokugawa Shogunate. The decaying government, they believed, was not equal to the task of facing the Western imperialism that threatened their country. Instead, they would restore direct imperial rule and create a new government that could face the Western challenge and preserve Japanese sovereignty. This event, the Meiji Restoration of 1868, revolved around the goals that would guide Japan through the first half of the twentieth century. Encapsulated in the Meiji slogan 'Rich Country, Strong Army,' these goals represented an effort to modernize and industrialize the country and to achieve equality with and acceptance by the West. This would be achieved largely by trying to emulate the West. With the 'restoration' of imperial rule, Japan, alone among the East Asian nations, implemented a thoroughgoing reform program that would enable it successfully to avoid Western domination. This Meiji 'Revolution' fundamentally altered the shape of the Japanese society, economy and government as well as Japan's position in Asia and the international community.

The great promise of Meiji was the creation of political democracy where none had existed before. The Meiji leaders, a young, energetic and ambitious group, outlined a series of reforms designed to strengthen Japan against the West, not to preserve Japanese culture, but to preserve the Japanese *nation*. To this end, they abolished the rigid traditional class system, which for centuries had divided society between the ruling samurai aristocracy and the subservient commoners. In the Imperial Charter Oath of April 1868, the new government promised that 'all classes high and low shall unite,' and be given the opportunity to 'fulfill their aspirations' (quoted in Schirokauer, 1978: 418). Land reform gave the peasantry title to the land they had worked for generations, and the freedom to grow whatever crops they chose. A new tax system, payable in money, relieved them of the need to grow rice and rice alone for payment to their daimyo overlords.[1] Education became compulsory: four years for boys *and* girls, later expanded to six years. A new banking system made low-interest loans available to entrepreneurs, and entrepreneurialism itself, for years despised as a mark of the lowly merchant class, was encouraged as a way to promote industrialization. The government also engaged in entrepreneurial activities, investing in and building industrial concerns like shipbuilding, mining, and chemicals manufacture, which it later sold off to private investors. Most promising to many was the prospect of a constitution, which the Emperor promised to his people in 1881. Constitutional government, many hoped, would bring democracy.

The real point of the Meiji Restoration, however, was not to establish political democracy. Democracy was instead merely a tool for building a strong state. The leading Japanese advocate of democracy in the early Meiji period was Fukuzawa Yukichi, who in the late nineteenth century wrote, 'The only reason for making the people in our country today advance toward civilization [*viz.* Western-style democracy] is to preserve our country's independence' (Fukuzawa, 1973: 151). In their quest to emulate Western strength, the Meiji leaders put in place the outward forms of democracy, but, intent on making rapid progress toward industrialization, they did not allow for true democratic expression. Democracy, after all, is a messy and time-consuming business. That the style, but not the substance of democracy was in place became most obvious in the 1890 Meiji Constitution, the document which would fundamentally shape the political order and political culture for the next five and a half decades. Debate between the Meiji leaders over whether to pattern the government on the English model, with a strong legislative branch and weak executive, or on the German model, with a strong executive and weak legislature, was the most divisive controversy of the Meiji period. Those who supported a more open, liberal government were defeated and forced to resign from the government.

The resulting Constitution, promulgated in 1890, created an extremely strong executive branch. The Emperor-centered document placed virtually no limits on imperial power: the Emperor could declare war, make peace, conclude treaties, and legislate by edict. The only check on imperial power was informal: while the Emperor – a youth of 16 at the time of the Restoration – had supreme authority according to the Constitution, it was understood by tradition and by the Meiji leaders that he would not exercise these powers on his own initiative.

Moreover, the Meiji system put the government into a precarious position *vis-à-vis* the military. A constitutional clause made the Army and Navy independent of civilian control, answerable only to the Emperor. But if the military was answerable only to the Emperor, and the Emperor was not expected to exercise power on his own initiative, who *was* in control of the military? As long as the civilian government was sound and functional, this question remained unasked and unanswered, but any crisis made the system vulnerable to the unilateral exertion of military power. On paper, the Emperor was all-powerful. In reality, he was not expected to act on this authority.

The first test of Japan's success in achieving its goals of 'Rich Country, Strong Army' came in the Sino-Japanese War of 1894–95. Viewing Korea as 'a dagger pointed at the heart of Japan,' the Japanese leadership focused on keeping Korea free from foreign domination. When China seemed poised to take a more prominent role in Korea, Japan initiated war. Victory over their vast continental neighbor, whose civilization the Japanese had admired (albeit grudgingly) for centuries, seemed to vindicate the tremendous change and sacrifice the Japanese had endured over the last generation. Fukuzawa, the Meiji liberal, wrote exultantly, but ominously, of the victory: 'Unimpassioned thought will show this victory over China as nothing more than the beginning of our foreign policy' (Fukuzawa, 1948: 359). In the peace settlement, Japan not only won a huge indemnity, which the government invested to spur industry, but also several territorial concessions, including the island of Taiwan, over which it established colonial rule in 1895. Following up this victory a scant ten years later with an even more surprising victory over Russia, Japan seemed destined for greatness, and a renewed sense of national pride began to take hold in Japan. At the same time, however, the Japanese became aware of Western racism as they confronted the wary Western response to their victory: as newspaper owner and former bureaucrat Ito Miyoji declared to a German friend, 'Of course, what is really wrong with us is that we have yellow skins. If our skins were as white as yours, the whole world would rejoice at our calling a halt to Russia's inexorable aggression' (quoted in Duus, 1976: 134). Increasingly, an 'us against them' mentality began to develop. In the aftermath of the Russo-Japanese War, Japan extended colonial control over Korea.

Thus, by early in the twentieth century, its empire now fortified with colonies in Taiwan and Korea, Japan seemed well on its way to securing its Meiji period goals. Industrial production continued apace, with significant cooperation between the government and the emerging entrepreneurial class. As Chalmers Johnson (1982) has noted, Japanese government and business shared similar goals. '[T]he secret of success in business,' declared one early Meiji businessman, 'is the determination to work for the sake of society and mankind as well as for the future of the nation, even if it means sacrificing oneself' (Morimura Ichizaemon, quoted in Marshall, 1967: 36).

For some, this sacrifice was more serious than for others. The growing demand for factory labor enticed many workers, male and female, off the farms. The resulting urbanization combined with Japan's growing international stature and the political reforms of Meiji to create an increasingly politicized population. While the government wanted a mobilized population, one that would work hard to achieve national goals, it could not

afford a restive and demanding population. In the early 1900s the government, concerned that the demands of a more sophisticated and politically
active population would threaten progress, enacted a series of social welfare
and labor laws, including a national health insurance law, child labor laws,
and labor mediation laws. This action, the government sponsors hoped,
would prevent the 'social diseases' they saw in the West, which they feared
carried the germ of revolution. The government made a preemptive strike,
but in doing so, robbed the people of the opportunity for political action
and retarded political development.

When World War I broke out in Europe in 1914, Japan, now clearly the
dominant nation in Asia, declared war on Germany and focused its
attention on the German-leased territories in China. Japan quickly occupied
the Shandong Peninsula, taking control of German-built mines, railroads
and other industrial concerns, and occupying German-held territories in the
Pacific. Without taking on any other significant military involvement
during the war, Japan was able to concentrate on supplying the other
combatants with war *matériel*, and enjoyed strong economic growth as
previously closed European and American markets opened up to Japanese
goods.

Concerned that Chinese weakness would threaten Japan (China's last
imperial dynasty fell in 1911) and eager to back up its military gains with
written agreements, in 1915 Japan took advantage of the diversion of
international attention and issued the Twenty-One Demands to China. The
series of demands signified Japan's desire to establish itself on the Chinese
mainland, especially in the northern area, Manchuria, and called on China
to sign former German rights on the Shandong Peninsula over to Japan and
to extend to Japan further privileges in southern Manchuria and eastern
Mongolia. After an unsuccessful appeal to the preoccupied European
nations, China found no alternative but to sign what was in effect an
ultimatum. Japan received huge concessions in China. But the Chinese
government, which by the mid-1910s had fractured into warlordism, was
so unstable that it could offer little guarantee for Japan's ill-gained rights.
This would serve to heighten Japanese anxiety over China, an anxiety that
would continue to infect Japanese attitudes toward China in the coming
decades.

The economic growth of the World War I period was also a mixed
blessing, for it brought with it rampant inflation. Between 1914 and 1918,
rice prices in Japan quadrupled. In August 1918, high rice prices led to the
outbreak of rioting which unexpectedly spread across the country. In the
popular mind, the high rice prices resulted in part from the government's
stockpiling rice to provision troops for the anti-Soviet Siberian expedition,
launched in response to the Russian Revolution and designed to protect
Japan's interests in the Manchurian railway. To quell the rioting, the

government dispatched the police and army. Tens of thousands of the over 700,000 who participated were arrested, and some of those charged were sentenced to death. This episode showed the dangers that lurked in the confluence of domestic and foreign crises, and also provided a foretaste of the heavy-handed tactics the government would employ in the future to silence the population and keep it on the straight and narrow.

Again, in 1923, crisis would pull back the curtain to reveal the darker side of Japan's success. On 1 September of that year, a huge earthquake devastated the Kanto plain, on which Tokyo sits. The Kanto Earthquake, which ignited fires that swept across Tokyo, killed 106,000 people and injured another 502,000. In the midst of the confusion and chaos that followed the earthquake, rioting broke out as people lashed out in anger, frustration and grief. The target of this popular emotion was the Korean minority in Japan, whom many accused, with the aid of rumors spread by both the police and the media, of setting the fires and inciting the rioting. The government, on the other hand, used the opportunity provided by the chaos to round up hundreds of left-wing intellectuals and radical leaders, whom it suspected as vectors of revolution that threatened to derail Japan's national progress.

The round-up of radicals continued into mid-September; the government justified its actions by claiming that radical leftists had incited the Koreans to revolt. In one case, Osugi Sakae, a leading anarchist, his mistress, the feminist Ito Noe, and his six-year-old nephew were arrested, imprisoned, and murdered by Amakasu Masahiko, a captain in the military police. This particularly horrifying instance of police brutality would later reverberate in the debate surrounding universal manhood suffrage. Moreover, the effort to recover after the earthquake put heavy financial burdens on the nation. The earthquake and its aftermath not only foreshadowed things to come, but also proved to be a trigger for future events.

Thus Japan entered the mid-1920s as a nation in flux. In 1925, after years of agitation, the government finally answered popular political demands with the passage of a bill extending suffrage to all adult males. As counterbalance to this fourfold expansion of the electorate, however, the government also passed the Peace Preservation Law, which outlawed certain radical organizations and gave it a stronger hand with which to control the population. Clearly, Japan was poised between the promise of greater democracy for the people and the threat of greater control by the government. The battle between these two trends, begun with the opening of the Meiji period, would be played out over the course of the next two decades.

In an extension of the policies that had won both Taiwan and Korea as Japanese colonies, in the early 1930s and 1940s Japan practiced aggressive policies in Asia aimed at establishing Japanese control over the entire region, eventually moving into Manchuria, China, Indochina and beyond. These efforts put Japan on a collision course with the United States and led to Japan's 1941 bombing of Pearl Harbor and the subsequent Pacific War. As the war raged, the Japanese government imposed ever-tighter controls on its own population while extending despotic control over most of Asia.

After initial victories, however, Japan's war efforts bogged down. When the 'utter destruction' promised in the Potsdam Declaration was visited on Japan, no one, least of all the Japanese themselves, knew what the future held. The Allied Occupation set out, with characteristic American hubris, to remake Japan in its image, to demilitarize and democratize the country, putting in place a series of far-reaching reforms that included fundamentally altering the role of the Emperor and rewriting the Constitution, as well as enacting land and labor reforms. When the Occupation ended in 1952, Japan regained its sovereignty.

HISTORIOGRAPHICAL OVERVIEW OF MODERN JAPAN

In the late nineteenth and early twentieth centuries, young nationalists from all over Asia hoped to learn from the Japanese example of how to modernize a nation. Thousands of young men (and a few women) flocked to Japan to observe the many modernizing reforms that the Japanese government had put in place to strengthen and industrialize their country. For these young people, Japan was a model for Asia. But from the perspective of Western historians studying Japan during the first half of the twentieth century (and there were very few), Japan's modernization was *sui generis*, completely unique, without precedent. Moreover, the process could not be replicated by the other 'backward' Asian nations.

The natural corollary of the interpretation of Japan's modernization as *sui generis* was that the process had not only been set in motion but had indeed been made possible by the arrival of the West in the form of US Commodore Matthew C. Perry in 1853. Without the arrival of the West, and without the subsequent 'assistance' and examples provided by the West, Japan's modernization would have been a non-starter, went this argument. Because the Japanese people were so adept at imitation, an art they had been perfecting since the early seventh-century adoption of Chinese ways, Japan was able to modernize successfully.

These views of Japan's modernization – that it was unique, that it was based primarily on Western contact – began to change around the end of World War II with the publication of a seminal work by Canadian historian E. Herbert Norman in 1940. In this book, *Japan's Emergence as a Modern State*, Norman looked at trends and developments in Japan's traditional society that predated the arrival of the West by a couple of centuries. The actual beginnings of Japan's modernization could be traced back to indigenous developments in Japanese society such as the growth of a market economy, the spread of transportation and communications networks, and profound changes in the social order, developments that occurred over the course of the Tokugawa period, 1600–1868. Norman's scholarship shifted the focus away from the West as motive force in Japan's modernization.

The end of World War II ushered in a whole new generation of Western scholars on Japan, an ironic but natural result of the long years of war. This new generation of scholars observed the many changes in the postwar world, primarily the beginning modernization of many other undeveloped nations and, coupling these observations with Norman's scholarship, arrived at more refined interpretations of Japan's modernization process. Japan could now be viewed as an example of how the process of modernization might take place in a non-Western nation, and its experiences could be extrapolated to other non-Western societies undergoing modernization.

The modernization process is a difficult, painful one for any society. As Japan underwent the fundamental social, political and economic changes linked to industrialization, it inevitably lost much of its traditional culture. In the case of a non-Western nation, however, the cultural change is even starker, since as second-tier developers these nations inevitably borrow the more advanced technology of the industrialized nations. Consequently, the process happens much more rapidly and the social dislocation is much more severe. Japan's modernization as a non-Western nation made it an example of a 'late developer,' an interpretation that unites Norman's idea of the 'indigenous' roots of modernization with the 'Western impact' interpretation. Since Japan had not been among the first tier of modernized nations, it had to 'catch up,' but it had an important head start in the industrialization process, because of the developments that had taken place during its traditional period. The Japanese fear was that if it did not catch up with the industrialized West, it would be overwhelmed, perhaps robbed of its sovereignty by the West. As a late developer, this interpretation runs, Japan had to develop very rapidly, or face the consequences. The government promoted the idea that achieving the twin goals of 'Rich Country, Strong Army' was imperative to the very survival of the nation, and brought intense pressure to bear on the Japanese people to work toward those goals for the national good. In this view, Japan's mobilization for war can be seen as an extreme example of the dislocation experienced by any society in transition.

However, this interpretation almost brings us back to the view of Japan as a model for modernization, a model for late developing non-Western nations. So, were those late nineteenth- and early twentieth-century Asian students correct in their assessment of Japan as a shining example? After the conflagration of World War II, when Japan unleashed its aggression on its Asian neighbors, few non-Japanese Asians could support the notion of Japan as model. Yet from the Western perspective, Japan seemed to be the storybook model of success: Japan's industrialization was rapid and so effective that it enabled Japan to assert itself militarily against its neighbors.

It was not until the mid-1980s and the early 1990s that Western scholars (in fact, the very scholars who had vaunted Japan's 'success') began to reassess Japan's record. Japan's modernization, they concluded, had been purchased at a great price. In Japan's rush to modernize, its rush to industrialize and build up its military, it exacted that price not only from itself, but from its neighbors. The most stunning example of the huge cost of Japan's modernization is, of course, the millions and millions of Asian lives that were lost in Japan's military aggression between 1894 and 1945. Between 1931 and 1945, Japan itself lost 3 million people in war. Throughout Asia, the United Nations estimates that as many as 19 million soldiers and civilians died as a result of Japan's aggression (Hane, 1996: 9). Millions of others, both in and outside Japan, suffered from the hunger, disease, homelessness and oppression created by Japan's warfare. Long after the physical wounds have healed, Asia suffers from the psychic and political effects of the years of war: mistrust and hostility still color the relationships between Japan and its Asian neighbors.

In another reckoning of price, Japan's 'success' in modernization must also be weighed against the fact that as the process was under way, the Japanese people were deprived of democratic freedoms. In its insistent push to modernize, the government denied the people their right to a voice. They were expected to work hard for national goals, and to subordinate their own demands to the demands of the state. The electorate was purposely limited to a tiny fraction of the population, and when it was finally expanded, the government enacted new laws to maintain strict control of the parameters of political activity and expression.

Along with industrial growth also came increasing disparities in economic growth. While city-dwellers prospered and benefited from the growing economy, the rural population suffered growing poverty and tenancy rates. The retarded growth of democracy and the economic disparities of industrial growth were issues the prewar and wartime Japanese government never dealt with. Only after the war were these issues addressed and remedies sought. Despite a lacklustre economy at the end of the twentieth century, Japan today seems on an even keel. Yet one must never forget the tremendous price that all of Asia, and indeed the Allied powers which fought the Pacific War, paid for the equilibrium.

Between 1925 and 1952, Japan underwent fundamental changes. While it is easy to divide modern Japan's history into 'prewar despotism and postwar democracy,' such a stark dichotomy is simplistic and negates the importance of studying history. To make sense of history, it is necessary to find the continuities that link prewar and postwar Japan. Thus during the war years, despotism and autocracy would be in the ascendant, as the Japanese government pursued aggressive policies in Asia and imposed repression at home. Japan achieved the national strength it had sought since the Meiji Restoration, but at the expense of freedom and democracy, not only in Japan, but in all of Asia.

Japan's activities in Asia during the 1925–52 period changed Japan and all of Asia in ways that continue to shape the world today. Communism spread in China, successful in large part because the Chinese Communists offered the most viable organization of anti-Japanese resistance. In Korea, the legacy of 40 years of Japanese colonial rule left the country divided, as Koreans struggled to establish self-rule. Vietnam, seized from French rule by Japan in 1940, also sought independence from its colonial overlords. And not least of all, changes wrought by the Allied Occupation locked Japan and the United States together as allies in the Pacific. Asia today is in many ways the result of Japan's late nineteenth- and early twentieth-century quest to secure its national sovereignty.

In one of history's great ironies, having lost the war, the Japanese won another chance to establish democracy in their nation. The Meiji goals of building a strong, independent nation, now on a sound democratic foundation, were achieved during the Occupation period. Thus Japan's Meiji era goals resulted not only in the pursuit of military aggression in Asia during the war years, but also, ultimately, in the emergence of a sound democracy in the postwar years. Though not apparently connected, these two trends both originate in the Meiji era effort to strengthen Japan internationally. Though despotism briefly and tragically triumphed, democracy ultimately emerged and it is on this basis that Japan has built its society in the last half of the twentieth century. The years between 1925 and 1952 constitute a critical link between the Meiji era goals gone awry and the ultimate emergence of democracy.

NOTE

1 Daimyo were feudal lords who controlled the some 240 *han* (domains) in Japan during the Tokugawa period. The administration of their domains was carried out by the samurai who served them.

PART TWO ANALYSIS

CHAPTER TWO

JAPAN IN 1925: A SOCIETY IN FLUX

By 1925 two generations of Japanese had lived through the flurry of fundamental social and political change inaugurated by the Meiji Restoration. It appeared that Japan's transition to modernity would continue apace into the next generations. Underlying Japan's government-directed transition to modernity was a deep-seated fear of Western domination. To face the foreign challenge, Japanese leaders had adopted many Western institutions, attempting to gain recognition from and equality with the powerful, industrialized Western nations. As a result especially of adopting Western political institutions, the Japanese population enjoyed more freedom than ever before. By the 1920s, the Japanese seemed more than ever to expect that freedom as a natural benefit of their commitment to national modernization. On the other hand, however, the Japanese government feared the implications of a nation of citizens voicing their individual demands. Consequently, by the mid-1920s a long simmering contest between greater democracy and greater government control was coming to a head. By the early 1930s, for reasons we shall examine later, the contest was settled on the side of government control.

The engine of national change was started by the government after the Meiji Restoration when it adopted plans for 'Rich Country, Strong Army,' the effort to build up Japan's economy and strengthen and modernize its military. By the mid-1920s, 'the modern sector of the economy was reaching maturity,' and Japan was a nation boiling with vitality and vigor, its society and culture displaying all of the vast changes that had taken place since the cataclysmic Meiji Restoration of 1868. 'Between 1912 and 1932, real national income per capita more than doubled, and living standards rose as well,' writes Peter Duus (1998: 185).

Those who benefited most from these rising standards, however, were Japan's urbanites. The demands of Japan's industrial revolution brought millions of Japanese to the cities to work in both the white- and blue-collar sectors, and as a result the urban centers saw huge growth. Even in the traditional period, Tokyo (then called Edo) had been a metropolis teeming with as many as 1 million people in the mid-eighteenth century. By the 1920s, Tokyo's population had more than doubled to 2.2 million. Osaka, Japan's second largest city, had a population of about 400,000 in the mid-eighteenth century; by the 1920s, it had mushroomed to 1.8 million people (Waswo, 1996: 59; Hunter, 1984: 231, 160). Similar patterns played out in other cities, primarily on the Pacific Ocean side of the islands, and in 1925 urban-dwellers constituted 21 percent of the population, or about 13 million out of a population of about 60 million. Most of this urban growth came as country people moved to the cities (Waswo, 1996: 57).

INDUSTRIALIZATION AND URBANIZATION

Rural-dwellers were drawn to the cities for employment opportunities in the factories that were opening up yearly. Most prominent in the early industrialization process was the textile industry, and most of the workers in this industry were young, unmarried women. Kenneth B. Pyle (1996: 152) writes that, 'The most distinctive feature of Japan's early industrialization was the critical role played by women in the labor force.' Indeed, up until the early 1930s, more women were engaged in factory employment than men, largely due to their dominance in the textile industry where they were sought-after for their small hands, their manual dexterity, and, one might assume, their traditional submission to authority. Female textile workers in the prewar period worked under strict control. They lived in dormitories, were not allowed to come and go as they pleased, and were subject to discipline that was frequently abusive. Many factory owners wanted to make the most of their costly equipment and kept the mills running 24 hours a day, requiring their employees to tend the machines in night and day shifts. Nevertheless, many women who worked in Japan's early textile mills agreed that this work was still easier than the back-breaking toil of the agricultural life (Hane, 1982: 173–204, 31). The pay-off for Japan was that 'By 1909 ... Japan had become the world's chief exporter of raw silk,' and 'by the 1920s Japan dominated the world market for cotton textiles' (Pyle, 1996: 154, 152).

While the textile industry paved the way, in order to achieve the government goal of 'Rich Country, Strong Army,' heavy industry was vital. In the 1870s, the government made huge investments to build shipyards, railroads, mines and chemical and munitions factories. In the 1880s, to forestall serious economic problems and curb inflation, the government launched a program of economic retrenchment and sold off these industries to private investors who achieved great success building on what the government had started. Heavy industry grew vastly during the World War I years, emerging for good and bad onto the world market.

LABOR UNREST

Japan's participation in the international market subjected the nation to global economic conditions. The economic boom of the World War I years brought hundreds of thousands of workers into the cities. With factories operating at capacity, labor became more valuable, and as a result the urban working class began to voice its demands. During the war years, the Yuaikai (Friendly Society), a labor organization founded in 1912 by Suzuki Bunji, became the leading force in the labor movement, growing more and more militant (Hunter, 1984: 107). This impetus toward labor militancy continued in the post-World War I years when the Japanese economy fell into a recession. In 1919, for example, 'the number of labor disputes sky-rocketed to 2388, five times as many as the year before' (Duus, 1998: 191). As Japan's recession continued into the early 1920s, a trend compounded by the massive destruction caused by the Kanto Earthquake of 1923, some 300 labor unions formed in response. Laboring men and women protested by participating in strikes and lock-outs. In 1921, for example, a massive strike by 30,000 shipyard workers in the Osaka–Kobe area shut down production for nearly two months (Duus, 1998: 191).

The government responded to labor unrest in a variety of ways. In 1911 the Diet passed a Factory Act designed to regulate and improve industrial working conditions by, for example, prohibiting employers from hiring children under 12 years of age and enforcing a 12 hour work day for women and workers under age 15. This Act, however, did not go into effect until 1916, and even then many of its provisions were never enforced. Moreover, the provisions applied only to factories employing 15 or more workers (Hunter, 1984: 41). More ominously, however, the government also tried to suppress labor demands with the police and even the military, and unions remained illegal throughout the prewar and war years. Fearing that labor unrest would derail the national goals, the government also attempted to co-opt the labor movement. Starting with the Factory Act of 1911, and continuing into the 1920s, the government enacted a flurry of legislation designed to stave off the 'Western disease.' This was what government leaders called the social fractiousness and individualism that seemed to characterize the Western democracies and which they feared would threaten Japan's goal-oriented cohesiveness. Expansion of the 1911 Factory Act in the 1920s mandated national health insurance and other social welfare provisions. But as Kenneth B. Pyle (1974) points out, the government's efforts were designed to mitigate the effects of industrialization most disruptive to the fabric of society, and most often tried to anticipate labor demands before labor itself got too heated in its protests. Thus the impetus for Japan's social legislation throughout the 1920s came not from the people, Pyle argues, but from a paternalistic government which enacted the laws as an attempt to control social change. In effect, the government was making a preemptive strike, and in doing so, robbed the population of the opportunity to become politically involved. In the end, this would have a retarding effect on democratic development.

URBAN CULTURE

As industrialization worked its changes and led to the development of an urban working class, so too did a new urban culture develop. Three things in particular helped to shape Japan's urban culture in the 1920s: the expansion of education that had occurred after the Meiji Restoration, Japan's increased contact with foreign nations, particularly with the West, and the impact of universal male military service.

Determining that an educated populace was a necessary prerequisite for the kind of economic and industrial growth Japan needed, in 1872 the Meiji government had enacted the Fundamental Code of Education, requiring all children (boys *and* girls) to attend school for four years. In 1907, the period of compulsory attendance was raised to six years, and by 1910 almost all children were completing the state-mandated education (Hunter, 1984: 29). It has been estimated that at the time of the Restoration, some 50 percent of the Japanese population had at least rudimentary reading skills, a figure that rose rapidly after the initiation of compulsory education.

Japan's literate population read voraciously. Newspapers and the popular press flourished during the Taisho period.[1] With 1,100 newspapers in circulation in 1920, estimates suggest that 'nearly half of the country's eleven million households subscribed to a daily paper' (Duus, 1998: 198). Also popular were magazines. Among the most widely read was *Kingu*, whose editor 'vowed it would become the most "entertaining, beneficial, cheapest and best-selling magazine in Japan."' *Kingu* contained stories of samurai heroics, sentimental romance, melodramatic events and action-packed drama. The editor attributed the magazine's success 'to the fact that he included articles that "were always a step behind the times"' (Hane, 1992: 225). Urban society was changing rapidly and the population at times yearned for the lost Japan.

But the Japanese public did not only indulge itself in looking back to a romanticized past. The existence of a larger reading public, along with technological advances, more highly developed managerial ability, and the growth of advertising, meant that the circulation of intellectual journals like *Kaizo*, *Taiyo*, and *Chuo koron* grew rapidly, even doubling in the early years of the twentieth century. While these 'general interest journals' wielded an influence on intellectuals and bureaucratic elites, Sharon Nolte (1987: 24) points out that 'even a fairly abstruse journal like *Chuo koron* could be seen in the hands of a worker or farmer during the Taisho era.' By 1919, the circulation of this journal had shot up from 5,000 copies to 120,000 copies. And the reading public did not just passively consume information. The *Yuai shinpo*, the journal of the labor organization Yuaikai, contained a section for readers' notes and comments and 'factory workers responded with a stream of observations and comments' (Hunter, 1984: 65).

The Taisho period also saw a rise in readership among women, particularly among the growing urban female middle class. This was reflected in the growth of such magazines for women as *Shufu no tomo* (The Housewife's Friend) and *Fujin koron* (Women's Review). Both publications contained information on child-rearing, household management and budgeting, and even articles on hard-to-manage mothers-in-law. *Fujin koron*, the weightier of the two, included debates on women's roles, working outside the home, and the status of the working woman. *Seito* (Bluestocking) was the publication of the women's organization Seitosha (Bluestocking Society), founded in 1911 by feminist Hiratsuka Raicho. The magazine, which at its peak sold some 3,000 copies per month, advocated female emancipation and social reform.

Continued contact with the West also influenced Japan's urban culture in the first decades of the twentieth century. Japan had opened itself to Western contact with the Meiji Restoration. Since the 1870s, hundreds of Western diplomats, industrialists and educators had spent time in Japan. Moreover, hundreds of Japanese had traveled outside Japan to observe the Western nations. In 1921, in an unprecedented move, Crown Prince Hirohito became the first member of Japan's imperial family to travel abroad. In a trip that took him to Great Britain and France, the Crown Prince set the tone for Japan's increased contact with the West in the 1920s. That the heir to the Chrysanthemum throne would travel to the West seemed to signify Japan's growing presence in the international community.

Japan's growing urban middle class was strongly influenced, at least superficially, by Western culture. Typifying the urban middle class was the white-collar worker, called a *salari-man*, or salaryman, Japan's version of the man in the gray flannel suit. The *salari-man*, who in the 1920s constituted about 5.5 percent of the employed population, or 1.5 million workers (Duus, 1998: 197), worked in a company, took home a regular salary, and generally enjoyed a secure, if somewhat rigid, work environment. Westernization took root in other ways as well. More and more people wore Western clothes in public, and many urban homes began to include Western-style rooms with carpets and curtains, easy chairs and coffee tables, bookshelves and floor lamps. Bread consumption rose.

Those who didn't care for gray flannel enjoyed Japan's version of the Jazz Age. Jazz was popular and most of the larger cities boasted dance halls where *mobos* and *mogas* ('modern boys' and 'modern girls') could be seen cutting up the dance floor, scandalizing their elders by dancing the foxtrot and the tango cheek-to-cheek.

Sports became popular during the Taisho period. Golf and tennis were for the ultra-chic, but most popular of all was *besu-boru* (baseball). The American pastime attracted a huge audience, and newspapers and large corporations contributed to the public enjoyment by sponsoring teams. Movies, too, became very popular, with Charlie Chaplin features competing for viewers with films like *Man-Slashing, Horse-Piercing Sword* (Duus, 1976: 187). In 1925, the government began regular radio broadcasts on government-owned stations, and listenership expanded rapidly; within three years, 500,000 households owned radios (Duus, 1998: 198).

Universal male military service also wielded a significant influence on the formation of Japan's early twentieth-century culture. In 1872 the Meiji leaders instituted conscription, and modeling the Japanese Imperial Army on Prussian and French models. All young men were required to serve for a period of three years. Yamagata Aritomo, a conservative nationalist who had been military leader of the Restoration forces and who is considered the 'architect' of Japan's modern military, called the Army a 'national university,' highlighting the important role the military played in shaping Japan's male citizens. In 1882, Yamagata wrote the Imperial Rescript to Soldiers and Sailors, a document designed to inoculate young servicemen with samurai ideals of self-sacrifice and loyalty to the Emperor. The Rescript was, of course, theoretically from the Emperor himself and its first article stated that 'The soldier and sailor should consider loyalty their essential duty.' The second article demanded that the soldier 'Regard the command of your superior officers as my [the Emperor's] command' (quoted in Irokawa, 1995: 133).

Training in the Imperial Army had paradoxical effects on young recruits. On the one hand, the Army reinforced ultra-traditional values. On the other, military service provided many young men with their first taste of things Western, introducing conscripts to 'trousers, jackets and boots as well as biscuits, beef and beer' (Waswo, 1996: 65). Also tremendously important was the fact that military service cut across class lines. Legal class distinctions had been abolished in the early Meiji period in an effort to create national unity and social cohesion, and to free all levels of society to work for the national goals. The military, then, was an institution that brought all levels of society together. Moreover, it was one of the only venues in which urban and rural society blended.

RURAL JAPAN

By the 1920s, Japan's development had created a huge gap between urban and rural society. It was as if there were 'two Japans,' writes Hane (1982: 33). And yet, the vast social and economic change taking place in the cities had occurred on the back of rural Japan. The strength of Japan's farming sector had provided the economic basis for the huge industrial and military growth over the Meiji period: between 1867 and 1875, the land tax provided 82 percent of the government's revenues, a figure which steadily declined as the industrial sector grew (Shibusawa, 1958: 410). The rural sector, however, saw little benefit from this growth and the gap between urban and rural life was vast.

As a result of this gap, rural-dwellers, still by far the larger segment of Japanese society, harbored deep resentment toward their urban counterparts. In 1925, Shibuya Teisuke, an organizer of the Agriculturists' Self-Rule Society, wrote:

> The cities grow more luxurious day by day ... while the villages have to live on moldy salted fish and wear shopworn clothes. And even these are not readily available to propertyless farmers, who are covered with dirt like moles and are suffocating in poverty like homeless mice. To begin with, the cities are living off the sweat of the farmers. They pilfer and live on what the peasants have produced with their sweat and blood. While the cities and city dwellers prosper, becoming daily more used to luxury, the peasants who labor to support and keep them alive are on the verge of starvation and death (quoted in Hane, 1982: 36).

Wrote Fukuzawa Yukichi in 1874, 'The purpose [of the government] seems to be to use the fruits of rural labor to make flowers for Tokyo' (quoted in Hane, 1982: 33).

Rural resentment was not just due to urban Japan's economic advantages, though that was an important factor. Urban wages were higher and consumer goods were more readily available, as were higher quality and more varied foodstuffs. The deepest resentment sprang from the fact that people in the countryside recognized quite clearly that their urban compatriots viewed them with snobbish contempt. A popular saying in the early twentieth century declared that 'an educated child [read 'urban'] turns up his nose at the privy back home' (Duus, 1998: 197). Moreover, urban Japan was largely unconcerned with rural poverty. Rural folks resented this disregard, and while on the one hand they envied urban advantages, they also excoriated the decline in traditional moral values that was evident in city life. For while society was changing rapidly in urban Japan in the early twentieth century, 'rural villages remained almost wholly unaffected by the changes until the end of World War II' (Hane, 1982: 34).

AGRICULTURAL LIFE

Despite the rapid changes in urban Japan, village life continued to revolve around wet rice agriculture. Thus the demands of the rice paddy molded the life of the family and of the community as a whole. The need to control precisely and calibrate the irrigation of the rice paddies, flooding them and draining them according to the life-cycle of the rice plant, required village-wide communication and cooperation. Failures on this count could result in disastrous harvests, so communal harmony was at a premium. Although village youth may have left their homes to serve in the Army or to seek work in the cities, 'most households stayed put, remaining in their village as far back as family memory stretched.' This created an extremely stable, if not stultifying, village community: 'Membership in the village was almost a birthright and villagers knew their neighbors' history as well as they knew their own' (Duus, 1998: 11). Novelist Tokutomi Kenjiro described this vividly:

> There's as much freedom in the country as in a prison, believe me. Drop a pebble in a bowl and you set up a tidal wave. Stretch your arms in the country and you bump old Tagobei's door – your legs, and they get caught in Gonsuke's back gate. If your daughter so much as changes the neckband of her kimono, the whole village must be talking about it. A hermit can live in the middle of any town, and in the capital nobody bothers about anything – but in the country you can't even sneeze without wondering what people will say (quoted in Duus, 1998: 11).

Rural women were expected to work in the fields as well as to take care of household matters. Marriages were arranged between families; after the wedding, women joined their husband's family and were absorbed into households in which two, three, or possibly more generations lived to-gether. The new bride was lowest in seniority, and as such was expected to perform back-breaking labor without complaint. One popular saying indicated that a 'wife shouldn't speak for the first fifteen years of marriage.' The mother-in-law finally had the opportunity to vent her bile for all the years she had suffered abuse from her own mother-in-law. No wonder many young women favored the harsh conditions of the textile mills over marriage in a rural village.

Though the new urban class might be tempted to romanticize the warm, all-encompassing nature of village life, in the 1920s rural poverty rates were growing. Urban industrial growth was rapid during World War I, but the war's end brought economic recession. The same pattern played out in the countryside as well. During the war, rice and silk prices rose, but after the war, economic problems rattled the foundations of village life. Rural youth who had traipsed to the city to find jobs during the boom years now returned to their villages where they became a burden on their strapped families. These already dire conditions only worsened in the 1930s when global depression set in. One historian estimates that in the prewar period, 'an average of 200,000 young girls were sold annually to serve as maids and nursemaids – a number exceeding the 179,000 women who became factory workers each year' (Irokawa, 1995: 8).

TENANT PROBLEMS

The activism that characterized urban labor in the mid-1920s made its way to the countryside as well, and was brought about in part by some of the same influences, for example universal education and the impact of military service. In traditional Japan, landlords had wielded great economic and social power in the countryside where the prevailing assumption was that 'men of wealth and position were morally superior to those of lower status.' Despite urban modernization, this assumption continued to shape social behavior in rural Japan. Tenants were expected to display respect and loyalty toward their landlords. They were expected, for example, to be available to perform labor for their landlords even if it meant being called away from their own fields (Waswo, 1996: 66). On the other hand, this paternalistic approach meant that landlords often felt an obligation toward their tenants, setting aside a portion of their wealth to provide relief in poor harvest years.

By 1907, as much as 45 percent of the cultivated land was worked by tenants (Hunter, 1984: 225). Most significant to landlord–tenant relations was the growing percentage of absentee landlords. As industrialization and urbanization became more widespread, and the cities began to offer more economic opportunities, more and more landlords began to move to the cities, a trend that accelerated after World War I. The trend toward absentee landlords weakened traditional community ties. During the early 1920s as the post-World War I recession set in, tenants began to organize into tenant unions and between 1917 and 1927 the number of such unions catapulted from 173 to 4,500, with a peak membership of 365,000 (Duus, 1998: 194). The leader of one union summed up the popular sentiment: 'In the past, we thought that "our existence depended on the grace and favor of landlords"; now we realize that it is "our labor that enables the landlords to live"' (quoted in Waswo, 1996: 67). In 1924 the government tried to respond to the growing rural discontent by enacting the Tenancy Arbitration Law, under which local officials and sometimes even the police mediated in disputes. Nevertheless, disputes tended to be settled in favor of the landlord (Hunter, 1984: 225).

In many ways rural Japan proved to be the breeding ground for the ultra-nationalism and militarism that would take over Japan in the 1930s and early 1940s. The economic suffering of rural Japan might have been more bearable had the rural community not felt that their taxes and labors were being used to support and benefit their urban compatriots. This rural resentment helped to fuel a growing cultural gap, and rural disgust about perceived urban individualism and materialism. To endure the economic problems and to give themselves a leg up on urban Japan, rural-dwellers began to emphasize traditional values, and a return to the purported 'Japanese spirit' of yore. It was among this population that Japan's military planners would find a fount of enthusiastic support for expansion and aggression in the 1930s.

NOTE

1   'Taisho' was the reign name of Emperor Yoshihito, who ascended the throne on the death of his father, the Meiji Emperor. Eras in modern Japan are referred to by the name of the imperial reign, thus the Meiji era lasted from 1868 to 1912; Taisho from 1912 to 1926; Showa from 1926 to 1989. The current period is referred to as Heisei, 1989 to the present.

CHAPTER THREE

DOMESTIC AND INTERNATIONAL TENSIONS, 1925–30

With the stroke of a pen, the 1925 passage of the Universal Manhood Suffrage Law instantly expanded the Japanese electorate nearly fourfold. Just ten days earlier, the Diet had laid the groundwork for this 'leap in the dark' (Premier Kato Komei, quoted in Duus, 1976: 170) by enacting the Peace Preservation Law, which strictly limited the public's right to engage in free and open political discourse. The nearly simultaneous passage of these two landmark bills encapsulated the contradictions inherent in the Meiji reforms, now over 50 years old, and set the tone for the decade to come. By the end of the 1920s, the government's dilemma, left over from the Meiji era, of engaging public commitment to the common cause while at the same time limiting the opportunities for public expression, would be resolved in favor of repression. As the nation neared the end of the 1920s, the intersection of crises both foreign and domestic made democracy seem just too dangerous, too serious a threat to Japan's security in a changing world.

By the mid-1920s, Japan could rightly claim to be the strongest nation in Asia. The Meiji goals of strengthening the nation militarily and industrially had largely been accomplished, and Japan had every reason to believe that it had finally arrived as an equal member of the international community, a community long dominated by the Western nations. Yet troubling blips on the screen signaled that perhaps all Japan had worked for was not as secure as it might be.

In 1924, after years of moving in this direction, the US Congress unilaterally enacted the Exclusion Act, which severely limited the number of Japanese allowed to settle in the United States. Just 15 years earlier, Japan, in a humiliating move to stop such formal action on the part of the United States, had entered into the 'Gentlemen's Agreement,' whereby it agreed to place restrictions on the numbers of Japanese emigrating to the US. The Exclusion Act thus came as a slap in the face and prompted the outbreak of anti-American demonstrations throughout Japan. The racial undertones in international relations apparent to some perceptive Japanese after the

Russo-Japanese War now became a resented fact of life for a much broader spectrum of the population.

That such an event would provoke political demonstrations was typical of Japan in the mid-1920s. This was the culmination of the period of so-called 'Taisho Democracy.' Throughout the 1910s and early 1920s, people at all levels of society had become more politically involved. The labor movement was at its prewar peak during the Taisho period, as was the women's movement. Even the outcaste *burakumin* organized an emancipation movement in the early 1920s.

UNIVERSAL MANHOOD SUFFRAGE AND THE PEACE
PRESERVATION LAW

Agitation to expand the electorate was part and parcel of this increased political activity. The Meiji Constitution of 1890 granted suffrage only to men who paid over 15 yen in annual taxes, an electorate that encompassed a mere 5 percent of the total male population (Pyle, 1996: 123). As early as 1892, a movement to expand suffrage was under way, a call that continued throughout the rest of the 1890s and into the first decades of the twentieth century. In 1911, the lower house of the Diet passed a universal manhood suffrage bill, only to have it rejected by the upper House of Peers. Finally, in 1925, after repeated attempts, the Diet passed the Universal Manhood Suffrage Law, granting the vote to all non-indigent men over the age of 25. The electorate instantly jumped from 3.3 million to 12.5 million. (Japanese women did not obtain the right to vote until after World War II.)

A dramatic turn in the struggle for voting rights had come in late 1923, in the chaotic wake of the Kanto Earthquake. In December, Namba Taisuke, son of a Diet member, attempted to assassinate Crown Prince Hirohito in retaliation for the post-Kanto Earthquake police murder of anarchist leader Osugi Sakae. The assassination attempt on the Crown Prince, regent for his father (the mentally unstable Emperor Yoshihito) since November 1921, badly shook the government and prominent members of the Diet voiced demands for increased vigilance against 'dangerous thought.' Putting action to their words, several of these Diet members founded the Kokuhonsha (National Foundation Society) in early 1924. The Kokuhonsha was a conservative organization that promoted Japanese nationalism, including ideas of Japan's unique character and its mission in Asia. This organization would eventually claim a membership of over 200,000, and was an important font of right-wing nationalist thought at the highest levels of government.

The attempt on the regent's life also galvanized action that would lead to the passage of the universal suffrage bill. Governmental leaders hoped the universal suffrage law would corral popular political energy into a sanctioned outlet and sap the attraction of the more radical options. In fact, however, the suffrage law became possible only because ten days earlier, in response to conservative elements such as the organizers of the new Kokuhonsha, the Diet had passed the Peace Preservation Law, a clear response to the fears aroused by the assassination attempt. The Peace Preservation Law made illegal any organization that advocated changing the *kokutai*, that is, the imperial system of government, or any organization that advocated ending the system of private property. The latter clause was clearly aimed at communists (Japan had just established diplomatic relations with the Soviet Union) but the vague wording of the bill gave radicals in general reason to fear. The law was not rescinded until after World War II; in fact, in 1941 it was strengthened to allow 'preventative arrest.' Indeed, over the years, nearly 70,000 people were arrested under this law, which was invoked especially in times of national distress.

One of the first periods of distress following the enactment of the law came in 1927 when investigations revealed that banks throughout Japan had incurred huge sums of unsecured debt. This resulted in a run on banks that led to the collapse of over 20 of them. This financial crisis was yet another of the aftershocks of the 1923 earthquake, since the huge government expenditures required for recovery had led to inflation and the weakening of the yen. The 1927 financial crisis resulted in a recession from which Japan was still struggling to recover when the 1929 collapse of the US stock market signaled the beginning of a global depression.

It was under these economic conditions, which inevitably led to increased political agitation by leftists and radicals, that the first election under the new suffrage law was held in February 1928. Prime Minister Tanaka Giichi, attempting to influence the outcome of the election, invoked the Peace Preservation Law to try to eliminate communist candidates from the ballots. Nevertheless, the election brought eight socialists to the Diet. Though these new Diet members had received a mere 5 percent of the popular vote, the government was alarmed, and Tanaka ordered the arrest of all suspected anarchists and communists. The result was a police sweep in mid-March 1928, which netted over 1,000 arrests and led to the dissolution of three leftist political parties. In the aftermath of the arrests the government also targeted academia, forcing the ouster of five left-leaning professors, including Kawakami Hajime, a Marxist economist at the prestigious Kyoto University. Moreover, after the 1928 round-up of leftists, a network of police remained in place to conduct surveillance throughout the country. And when the Diet declined Tanaka's call to amend the Peace Preservation Law to allow for the death penalty, Tanaka had it amended by imperial decree.

Tanaka Giichi (1863–1929) was born a member of the samurai class just five years before the Meiji Restoration. He was a Military Academy graduate who served in the Army and did active service in Manchuria during the Russo-Japanese War. A strong advocate of inculcating youth with martial values, in 1910 he helped his mentor, Meiji military architect Yamagata Aritomo, to establish the Imperial Reservists' Association. The Reservists' Association operated as a propaganda machine to promote the popularity of the military by sponsoring various patriotic ceremonies and drills at which it preached nationalist ideology: 'Japan's thousands of hamlets [would be] the army's agrarian cells' (quoted in Hane, 1982: 60). Tanaka served as War Minister in 1918–21 and again in 1923–24. When in 1927 the heat of the financial crisis brought the fall of the Wakatsuki Cabinet, Tanaka became Prime Minister.

CHINA PROBLEMS

As Prime Minister, Tanaka's strong-arm tactics in domestic policy were replicated in foreign policy. Like most in the military, Tanaka was concerned that Chinese instability was a threat to Japan's Asian interests, which included its colonies in Korea, Taiwan, and concessions in Manchuria: the South Manchurian Railway, the Hanyehping iron and coal works and access to other natural resources.

After the fall of the Qing Dynasty in 1911, China had seen the brief presidency of Sun Yatsen. Because he lacked military power, Sun turned over the presidency to the former Qing general, Yuan Shikai. Yuan Shikai's imperial dreams died with him in 1916 and the country, lacking any sound foundation for republican government, fell into a period of warlordism. During this time of political chaos, the Chinese Communist Party (CCP) was founded; it vied for legitimacy with the Guomindang (GMD) Nationalist Party, led by Sun Yatsen. In 1923, Sun, believing that an end to warlordism was in the interests of both the CCP and the GMD, negotiated a united front with the Communists to wipe out the warlords and reunite the country. When Sun died after a brief struggle with cancer in 1925, Chiang Kaishek, head of the Whampoa Military Academy, assumed leadership of the GMD and the united front. The following year Chiang launched the long-awaited Northern Expedition to reunite the country.

Japanese leaders, who had viewed prior Chinese instability with a wary eye, were even more alarmed by the prospect of a newly strong and unified China. When Chiang lashed out against the united front's Communist element in Shanghai and declared the founding of a new Nationalist government in Nanjing, the Tanaka Cabinet responded by sending the Shandong Expedition to China in the summer of 1927. Though ostensibly to protect Japanese citizens in the face of renewed anti-Japanese demonstrations (which had been recurrent since Japan's 1915 issuance of the Twenty-One Demands), the Expedition in fact lent support to Manchurian warlord Zhang Zuolin (Chang Tso-lin). Though Chiang temporarily halted his campaign after capturing Nanjing, the possibility of a continued Nationalist advance northward threatened the Manchurian interests of both Zhang and the Japanese.

The Shandong Expedition was the bailiwick of the Kwantung Army, named after the province in Manchuria to which they were first sent to guard Japanese interests in 1907, two years after Japan's victory in the Russo-Japanese War. The Kwantung Army consisted of a single division whose mission was to protect Japanese citizens in the Manchurian area as well as the Southern Manchurian Railway and the Japanese-leased areas of Manchuria, and had enjoyed independent status since 1919. As an elite force, the Kwantung Army attracted highly motivated young officers. Many of these young officers came to believe that they possessed a unique understanding of Japanese interests in Manchuria, and the Kwantung Army became a leading advocate of an assertive Japanese policy in this resource-rich Chinese province, regarded by many Japanese as their nation's new 'frontier' (see, for example, Seki, 1984).

Having sent troops to guard the Shandong Peninsula against Chiang Kaishek's reunification campaign, Tanaka opened the Eastern Conference at which top military and foreign office officials were invested with the task of defining Japan's policy toward China. What emerged was the so-called 'Positive Policy,' Tanaka's statement that Japanese interests in Manchuria must be maintained as distinct from their interests in the rest of the country.[1] In other words, in the event that Chiang was successful in re-uniting the country under Nationalist rule, Manchuria must nevertheless be maintained under separate jurisdiction.

This policy eschewed the involvement of the international community in Japan's affairs in Manchuria. From the Japanese perspective, such things as the American Exclusion Act had threatened their place in the international community. The Western powers could not be trusted to understand Japan's unique needs and role in Asia, nor could they be expected to look out for them. As Shigemitsu Mamoru, wartime Foreign Minister (later convicted as a Class A war criminal), would explain in a postwar book, 'Manchuria was Japan's own particular problem, which could be settled only by Japan herself ... [Prime Minister Tanaka] ... maintained that as a practical policy towards China, Manchuria should be regarded as a special region of China and as such should have distinct treatment' (Shigemitsu, 1958: 43). In a number of important ways, as we shall see, it was Japan's policy toward Manchuria that led Japan into conflict with the Anglo-American powers.

Tanaka's Positive Policy was a move away from 'Shidehara Diplomacy' – the foreign policies pursued by Shidehara Kijuro, Foreign Minister under premiers Kato Takaaki and Wakatsuki Reijiro from June 1924 to April

1927. (He would serve in this position again in the Hamaguchi Cabinet, July 1929–April 1931, and the second Wakatsuki Cabinet, April 1931–December 1931.) Shidehara advocated non-intervention and non-expansion into China, instead promoting economic and diplomatic means to securing Japan's interests in China. It was this 'Shidehara Diplomacy' that was in effect rejected by the Eastern Conference. Shidehara was a professional diplomat, a law graduate from Tokyo University who served as ambassador to the United States in 1919–22. Shidehara's moderate position had earlier been damaged by his inability to forestall the American adoption of the Exclusion Act in 1924, and when Tanaka became Premier in April 1927, Tanaka himself also took over the post of Foreign Minister.

Thus the new direction in Japanese foreign policy represented by Tanaka's 'Positive Policy' was in large part a reaction to Japanese perceptions that their interests were increasingly threatened both by the racist policies of the United States and the West in general, and by the Chinese drive toward reunification. Shidehara's approach to resolving these problems had seemed predicated on an assumption that Japan could and should act as a member of the international community, or to use a phrase not contemporary to the times, as a member of the developed world. His experience as a diplomat would support this approach, but he could also bring more objective evidence to the argument. During the Meiji period Japan had made steady progress toward eliminating the unequal treaties it had been forced to sign with the Western powers. In July 1894, Foreign Minister Mutsu Munemitsu signed a treaty with England which ended extraterritoriality and put the two powers on an equal footing except for tariff autonomy. Soon after, other Western nations signed similar treaties with Japan. Tariff autonomy was achieved in 1911. Japan signed its first military treaty with England in 1902, when both nations, bound by mistrust of Russia, entered into the Anglo-Japanese Alliance. Moreover, Shidehara's experience as ambassador to the United States gave him a more international perspective, a belief that Japan must 'mak[e] use of co-operation and persuasion in the international sphere ... [and] act on the basis of mutual agreement' (Shigemitsu, 1958: 42).

But Shidehara diplomacy, writes Peter Duus (1976: 200), 'whatever its merits ... did not reflect a national consensus.' Japan's national consensus was informed, instead, by another body of evidence that felt more compelling to the broad spectrum of Japanese whose very society had been overturned by the events of the Meiji period. Overwhelmed by Western military power, Japan's weaknesses were glaring despite the nation's proud history. To strengthen their nation, they had abandoned much of their tradition and had achieved stunning success, which they had proved on the battlefields in their wars with China and Russia. For all their effort, however, many Japanese still felt slighted, looked down upon and condescended to. The Treaty of Portsmouth that ended the Russo-Japanese War, for example, had been met with popular rioting in Japan because it failed to deliver indemnities and a satisfactory territorial settlement. While World War I had opened markets traditionally closed to Japan, as soon as the war was over, the Western nations took up with their traditional trading partners and again excluded Japan. The Exclusion Act was just the latest installment in the West's record of rejection. So to many Japanese, Prime Minister Tanaka's more assertive foreign policy seemed a necessary protection of Japan's interests in Asia.

The first military test of the Positive Policy came in the summer of 1928. In March, Chiang Kaishek renewed his military campaign to reunify China by marching north to challenge Manchurian warlord Zhang Zuolin. Successful fighting brought his forces close to Zhang's base in Beijing. With Chiang poised to claim victory, the Tanaka Cabinet ordered more Japanese troops to the Shandong Peninsula. With some of these troops in place when Chiang entered Jinan (Tsinan), about 200 miles south of Beijing, negotiations commenced. In early May, however, Japanese and Chinese troops clashed and fighting broke out. This Jinan Incident led to an explosion of anti-Japanese sentiment in China, heightening Japanese insecurities about their position in China.

ARMY INSUBORDINATION: THE ASSASSINATION OF ZHANG ZUOLIN

The Tanaka Cabinet hoped that by helping Zhang Zuolin maintain an independent Manchuria, he would in return accept a Japanese presence there. The fact that they shared a common enemy in Chiang Kaishek was, however, a very shaky basis for an alliance between Japan and Zhang Zuolin, and despite their common interests, both sides naturally kept a wary eye on the possibility of a future showdown with one another. When the showdown came, it was neither planned nor led by the government in Tokyo. Instead, in what would become a devastating pattern of military insubordination, Colonel Komoto Daisaku, senior staff officer of the Kwantung Army,[2] plotted and carried out the assassination of Zhang Zuolin. Operating on the growing military belief that the civilian government was out of touch with the realities of the situation on the ground, Komoto planned to implicate the Chinese in the murder and hoped the government in Tokyo would respond to the instability by expanding their military role and establishing Japanese dominance in the area.

With the aid of a demolitions expert brought to the job from nearby Korea, Komoto and his conspirators, other staff officers in the Kwantung Army, planned to explode Zhang's private railcar. Having practiced on two other bridges in the previous month, they laid the explosives on a bridge just outside Mukden on the morning of 4 June 1928. To lend authenticity to the claims that the Chinese were responsible, the plan also called for killing three Chinese vagrants ostensibly found in guerrilla dress.

The bomb exploded on cue and killed Zhang instantly. The government in Tokyo, thoroughly shaken by the news, refused to take military or political advantage of the calamity. Despite press censorship designed to keep the story out of the newspapers – the event was described as 'a certain serious incident in Manchuria' (quoted in Coox, 1989: 406) – the story emerged, possibly from one of the Chinese vagrants who escaped his captors. As the news leaked out, it crippled the Tanaka Cabinet, which was forced to resign the following year.

Very soon, the ironic results of the dramatic incident would become apparent. Domestically, the fall of the Tanaka Cabinet led to the elevation of Hamaguchi Osachi as Prime Minister. Hamaguchi's background was in finance, and he had served earlier as Finance Minister. Hamaguchi brought back Shidehara Kijuro as Foreign Minister. The Hamaguchi Cabinet would govern Japan for nearly two years, from July 1929 to April 1931. (Shidehara served as acting Prime Minister from November 1930, but more on this later.) The new administration thus offered a stark contrast to Tanaka's, and it was a contrast the military was not happy about. Instead of Tanaka's Positive Policy toward China, Hamaguchi and Shidehara reintroduced the earlier conciliatory approach to foreign relations, especially relations with China. Rather than using its military might, under the Hamaguchi Cabinet Japanese policy was to secure its interests in China through peaceful economic and diplomatic means.

The irony of Zhang's assassination was apparent not only domestically, but in events in China as well. Komoto and his Kwantung Army conspirators had assumed that with the powerful Zhang out of the way, his power base in Manchuria would crumble. Zhang's son, Zhang Xueliang (Chang Hsueh-liang), was a known womanizer and opium addict, clearly not a serious threat to Japanese interests. But his father's murder at the hands of the Japanese galvanized the 'Young Marshal,' and within six months he announced his allegiance to Chiang Kaishek and the Nationalists, joining his considerable forces to those already arrayed against Japan.

The assassination of Zhang Zuolin thus resulted in the very things the military planners most feared: a domestic government that was conciliatory toward China, and a more unified China. This, however, was the most significant punishment the conspirators received. The army was secretive about its review of the incident, and the conspirators, never charged with the murder, remained in their positions. How could such a serious act of military insubordination go unpunished? The fact that it did revealed the growing weakness of the civilian government *vis-à-vis* the military. In part, this weakness was written into the Meiji Constitution. According to the

Meiji Constitution, the military enjoyed what was called the 'Independence of the Supreme Command': neither the Diet nor the Cabinet held any authority over the military, which was answerable only to the Emperor. In military matters, the definition of which expanded gradually over the course of the early twentieth century, the military was able to bypass the Cabinet and report directly to the Emperor. In 1900 an additional ordinance stipulated that the ministers of war and of the navy come from the ranks of generals and admirals on active service. Because an incomplete Cabinet could not stand, this ordinance gave the military the power to bring down a Cabinet through resignation or by refusing to appoint a minister (or by threatening either action).

This had not emerged as a problem earlier because both the Cabinet and the military were controlled by the same small group of men. But as this group of men, the leaders of the Meiji Restoration, passed from the scene, the military and the civilian arms of government became more divergent and the military was increasingly able and inclined to interfere in politics. During the early years of the twentieth century, the military had steadily grown in influence, aided by such things as the Imperial Reservists' Association. By 1925, however, the Army suffered a reduction of four divisions, down to 17, a cut of about 35,000 men. This was accompanied by budget cuts. Military cuts were an outgrowth of Shidehara's diplomatic policies and international arms agreements, but they caused great discontent in the Army and Navy, which seethed with resentment. Nor were the military cuts popular with the Japanese people. In the political bargaining that surrounded the military cutbacks, War Minister Ugaki Kazushige (1924–27) was able to introduce military training for all students from middle school up, as well as a reorganization of reservist units in factories and villages throughout the country. Thus even as the military suffered cuts in the mid-1920s, its popularity was growing throughout the nation. This, coupled with a growing perception that Japan was being pressed from the outside, especially by events in China, ultimately created a hothouse environment for military growth.

NAVAL ARMS LIMITATION TALKS

The unpopularity of the military cuts was dramatically expressed in the sharply negative reaction to the 1930 London Conference agreements on naval arms limitations. In 1921–22, in the aftermath of World War I, the Great Powers had convened the Washington Conference to address the naval arms race that was developing between Great Britain, the United States, and Japan. After the war, Japan's Imperial Navy had hoped to build a naval force equal to 70 percent of that of the United States, which would give it superiority over the American Pacific Fleet in the waters surrounding

Japan. Japan's delegate to the conference was Shidehara Kijuro, who was then serving as Ambassador to the United States. At the conference, Japan agreed to relinquish some of the gains it made in China during World War I, including its acquisitions in the former German territories on the strategically located Shandong Peninsula, in exchange for Chinese recognition of Japan's economic interests there. Moreover, in the Nine Power Treaty, Japan agreed (along with Britain, France, the United States, Italy, Portugal, Belgium, Holland and China) to respect 'the sovereignty, the independence, and the territorial and administrative integrity of China' (quoted in Spence, 1990: 379). (The Western powers did not, however, relinquish the concessions from China they had enjoyed for the last 70 years, via the unequal treaties.)

The main focus of the Washington Conference, however, was on naval arms limitation and creating a naval balance of power. The central treaty of the conference, the Five Power Treaty, set a tonnage ratio of 10:10:6 for battleships and aircraft carriers for Great Britain, the United States, and Japan. (France and Italy completed the 'five powers,' signing on with a ratio of 1.75 each.) Japan was willing to drop its demand for a 10:10:7 ratio, because both Great Britain and the US agreed that they would not build any new fortifications east of Pearl Harbor (with the exception of Australia and New Zealand for Great Britain). In any event, the final agreement provided the Japanese with a naval capacity equivalent to the strength of the combined Pacific fleets of Great Britain and the US and sufficient for protecting their four home islands and colonial possessions. 'The consensus of naval opinion was that … the treaty … gave the Japanese an unchallengable control in East Asian waters' (Tiedemann, 1984: 5).

Most people in Japan were generally satisfied with the agreement, feeling that the resulting accords acknowledged Japan's security needs in the Pacific. The Japanese reaction to the London Conference treaties eight years later, however, was vastly different, and highlighted the shifts in domestic political attitudes and in the military's political power that had taken place over the course of the 1920s. The differing reactions to these two naval arms limitations treaties highlights the sea change Japan experienced in public (and military) attitudes toward both domestic politics and international relations over the course of the 1920s.

The London Conference of 1930 was designed to update the agreements of the Washington Conference. By the end of the 1920s Japan's heightened concern over China prompted demands for an expanded tonnage ratio *vis-à-vis* the Western powers. Though the Tanaka Cabinet had fallen in 1929 in the aftermath of Zhang Zuolin's murder, the military in general held fast to the defense policies Tanaka had outlined. The Navy in particular now considered a 70 percent ratio, which Japan had surrendered at the Washington Conference, to be *de rigeur*. A 70 percent ratio, Navy

Chief of Staff Admiral Kato Kanji told Prime Minister Hamaguchi, 'is the absolutely lowest ratio and is a matter of life and death for our navy. If an agreement for that ratio is not secured, we must resolutely break off negotiations' (quoted in Kobayashi, 1984: 29).

What emerged from the conference, however, was a British and American demand that in essence the 5:5:3 ratios established at Washington be maintained. After intense negotiations, the formula agreed upon allowed Japan a 70 percent ratio until 1936, after which time the 5:5:3 ratio would again come into effect. Prime Minister Hamaguchi signed the treaty over the intense opposition of the Navy General Staff, who feared that it would fatally weaken Japan's strength in the Pacific. Challenging the authority of the civilian government to make such a decision, Admiral Kato resigned over the issue, and the Navy General Staff, exercising the right of the 'independence of the supreme command,' registered their complaints directly with the Emperor. The appeal was also made in the press, and the Navy won much support for their view in the popular mind. Though the London Naval Treaty stood as ratified, Hamaguchi made concessions to the Navy, removing officials who supported the treaty from the Navy Ministry and agreeing in future to closer consultation with the military general staffs. The concessions, though moderate, symbolically strengthened the Navy, and by extension the Army, *vis-à-vis* the civilian government, and the treaty controversy gave rise to deep resentments.

That resentment would erupt into violence when early in the morning of 14 November 1930, Prime Minister Hamaguchi was gunned down at Tokyo Station by Sageo Tomeo, a member of the right-wing patriotic organization the Aikokusha. Mortally wounded, Hamaguchi died ten months later. The decade whose mid-point saw the vast expansion of the electorate would end in violence, with an assassination perpetrated by a defender of the military, that ushered in an era of politically motivated assassinations and military adventurism. The next decade would bring the increasing militarization of civil society, played out against a backdrop of global economic troubles and insecurities over China. The dilemma between popular participation in government and authoritarian control of the nation was being resolved in favor of government control, by a government that was increasingly dominated by the military.

NOTES

[1]   For many years scholars debated about the so-called 'Tanaka Memorial,' supposedly a secret report Prime Minister Tanaka issued to Emperor Hirohito as a result of this conference that outlined Japanese plans for world conquest in which he argued that the first step toward this goal would be conquering Manchuria. Reputable scholars now view this so-called 'Tanaka Memorial' as bogus, though some argue it may have existed as a Russian forgery.

2   Alvin D. Coox (1989: 406) writes: 'The suspicion could never be laid to rest that at least the Kwantung Army commander, Muraoka Chotaro, and perhaps his chief of staff, Saito Hisashi, were indirectly involved, and that Komoto was acting at the behest of his superiors.'

CHAPTER FOUR

JAPAN'S 'MISSION IN ASIA'

Prime Minister Hamaguchi's physical deterioration after receiving a bullet wound at the hands of a right-wing assassin presaged the deterioration of civilian government in Japan during the first half of the 1930s. This assassination would prove to be the first act in a drama one historian has called 'government by assassination,' as the military involved itself in politics and endeavored to restore the direct imperial rule they believed was essential to protect and promote Japan's increasingly threatened security interests (Byas, 1942). Between 1931 and 1936, the authority of the civilian government was steadily eroded by the military. Against a backdrop of global economic woes and growing instability in China, Japan's military took a firmer grip on the reins of power. By 1932, Japan had extended its control over Manchuria and four years later was on the brink of war with China.

ECONOMIC DEPRESSION

The events of the early 1930s played out against a backdrop of social instability produced by severe economic difficulties. In the trajectory of industrialization, Japan during the late 1920s and early 1930s was in the 'take-off' period. This was the transition from agriculture and light industry to heavy industry, from a predominantly agricultural labor force to an industrial workforce, a phase that has been called the 'most difficult and precarious phase in the course of a country's modernization' (Kosaka, 1992: 28).

Difficult in its own right, this phase coincided with problems brought on by Japan's involvement in the international economy. During World War I Japan enjoyed great economic growth as it broke into previously closed markets and supplied the combatant powers with war *matériel* and other goods. But these markets closed again when the war ended, and just as Japan was recovering from this economic downturn the Kanto Earthquake struck. The recovery efforts placed a devastatingly high demand on Japan's economy. Yet recovery was again in sight by the end of the 1920s. By late 1929, the Hamaguchi Cabinet's Financial Minister, Inoue Junnosuke, finally returned Japan to the gold standard, which it had gone off in 1917 when the gold embargo was imposed. This attempt to stabilize the yen, put off many times over the course of the 1920s, was aimed at increasing foreign trade. But it came at exactly the wrong time, just weeks after the collapse of the US stock market in October 1929. As a result, the effects of the Great Depression hit Japan all the more severely, with an impact that reverberated throughout all levels of the economy.

A look at the silk industry illustrates the dire economic situation of the early 1930s. Silk exports had led Japan's industrial transformation; soon after the stock market crash, American imports of silk all but halted. By 1930, the price of silk cocoons was 80 percent below the 1925 price. This hit the agrarian sector hard, and farm family incomes dropped from the 1926 index of 100 to 33.5 by 1931 (Hane, 1982: 114, 278–9). In a grisly account of rural conditions in 1932 novelist and reporter Shimomura Chiaki recorded his winter-time conversation with a peasant man:

> This could turn into a blizzard. On top of the famine, if we get a blizzard that lasts three days, all the farmers in this region will starve to death. In the famine of the Tenmei era (1782–1787), they say 30,000 people starved to death. Those who survived ate human flesh. It was said that the flesh of girls between seventeen and eighteen years of age was the best, so they waited for such girls to die and ate their flesh. If we don't watch out, we'll see the same thing happening this year. A famine like this shows that the end of the world is at hand.

An elderly woman listening nearby responded:

> About what the man was saying … it wasn't only the people of olden days who ate flesh. We too are eating the flesh of human beings. In order to make it possible for the children to survive, we have to feed them their parents' flesh. To make it possible for the parents to survive, we have to eat the children's flesh. So, right now I am trying to stay alive by eating my daughter's flesh (quoted in Hane, 1982: 130, 131).

Though also hard hit by the depression, urban Japan fared better than rural Japan. Continuing a trend that had begun during the Meiji era, peasants poured into the urban areas seeking work. Once in the city, their anti-urban resentments were fueled by the sight of their relatively better-off brethren, and by the attitude of condescension they met as they wandered the confusing streets of Japan's sprawling cities. Their resentments were also fed by a widespread feeling that their miserable conditions were not only of no concern to city-dwellers, but that their problems were exacerbated by corporate business, and by corrupt politicians in the government. These resentments were trumpeted by right-wing organizations, which excoriated the self-serving behavior of the industrialists and politicians.

In this climate of economic despair and political decline, the military emerged as a seemingly shining and pure example of the true spirit of the nation. Aided in part by decades of indoctrination, the military found its most fervent support in the down-trodden rural areas. For many rural youths, military service was the ticket out of poverty and degradation. Military leaders and organizations like the Imperial Reservists' Association promoted the idea that the 'soldiers were the arms and legs of the empire ... better than civilians.' Young peasant men struggling to survive 'consider it the greatest honor attainable, once they enter the army, to become a private superior class [a rank below that of corporal],' related one observer in 1929. 'All the villagers share this view. As the young recruits leave the village, they all vow to come back as private superior class' (Yuki, 1935: 27).

MANCHURIAN INCIDENT

The prestige of the military in the popular mind and the attitude of superiority among the military itself contributed to the military's growing sense of independence. This independent military exploded into action in the evening of 18 September 1931. In an episode strongly reminiscent of the assassination of Zhang Zuolin three years earlier, field grade officers of the Kwantung Army exploded a bomb on a section of the South Manchurian Railway just north of Mukden. Although the 'Young Marshal,' Zhang Xueliang, had confined his forces of some 10,000 Chinese troops to their barracks precisely to avoid confrontation with Japanese troops, which were on maneuvers in the area, the Japanese officers blamed the bombing on the Chinese. Within a few hours of the incident, soldiers of the Kwantung Army, claiming they were acting in self-defense, opened fire on the Young Marshal's barracked troops. Shortly after, the Mukden region's senior Japanese staff officer ordered Japanese troops to occupy nearby Mukden. Acting in concert with the conspirators but independent of the Japanese government, the Japanese commander in Korea sent in reinforcements from Japan's Korean colony, just to the south. The Army's actions were stunningly effective. Nationalist leader Chiang Kaishek, troubled by crises of his own, decided he could not expend any of his resources on defending Manchuria and ordered Zhang Xueliang not to put up any resistance. Within days the Kwantung Army had established control over most of Manchuria.

All was done without instruction, indeed in spite of instruction, from the civilian government in Tokyo. The main players in the plotting were Lieutenant-Colonel Ishiwara Kanji, Colonel Itagaki Seishiro, and Colonel Doihara Kenji. These men typified the military belief that the military alone understood the gravity of Japan's interests in Manchuria. The civilian government, they believed, was ignorant and out of touch with the reality of the situation. The day after the incident, Kwantung Army Commander-in-Chief Honjo Shigeru cabled Prime Minister Wakatsuki Reijiro's government in Tokyo, urging a military occupation of the region: 'This is the best moment to solve the Manchurian question. Should our army fail to grasp it and adopt a conservative attitude, it will forever become impossible to solve the question ... We hope you will make a grave resolution so that the entire army will march toward achieving the nation's fundamental and long-lasting goals' (quoted in Shimada, 1984: 255).

Despite having some prior knowledge of the plot, the Tokyo government proved incapable of reigning in the military, either before or after the incident. In fact, the staff officers in the field who planned the bombing – Ishiwara, Itagaki and Doihara – had carefully enlisted the tacit support of the general staff in Tokyo. When shortly before the incident Foreign Minister Shidehara got information that the Kwantung Army was moving troops and supplies to the area, he asked War Minister Minami Jiro to send a representative to Manchuria to assert control over the situation. Major-General Yoshitsugu Tatekawa, who supported the Kwantung Army's plot, arrived on the scene in mid-September, and spent the night of the incident in the company of geisha girls, allowing the scene to unfold as planned by the Army conspirators.

Unable to stop the plot before it broke out, the civilian government in Tokyo also proved impotent in its aftermath. On hearing news of the event, the Wakatsuki Cabinet's immediate reaction was to order the hostilities contained. But War Minister Minami was the effective (or ineffective) link between the Cabinet and the Kwantung Army, and his instructions were never delivered with force. The Army completely ignored the Cabinet's instructions. Indeed, day by day the line of Japanese advance pushed further and further. When even the Emperor indicated support of the Cabinet's call to limit the hostilities, Kwantung Army leaders, buoyed by the support of an enthusiastic public, railed against the traitorous advisors to the throne. Short of undertaking a bold purge of radical elements in the military, the Cabinet decided that the Emperor should best refrain from commenting on the issue.

The Army had won the showdown. Rather than lose face by revealing their own weakness, the Cabinet was now put in the position of explaining a situation they had had no role in planning to the international community. From this point forward, for the next 15 years, the military had effective control of foreign policy. Japan's control of Manchuria, 'a paradise and a treasure house – a source of raw materials, a safety valve for Japan's surplus population and unemployed, and a base for the development of heavy industry,' became the cornerstone of the nation's foreign policy (Coox, 1989: 426). The Manchurian Incident thus constituted, as Peter

Duus (1976: 205) has written, a 'diplomatic revolution.' It was, moreover, the beginning of Japan's drive for hegemony in Asia that directly led to the explosion of the Pacific War, a war which the Japanese call the 'Fifteen Year War.' As Tojo Hideki, who would become Japan's wartime Prime Minister, would reflect on the incident in 1941,

> The Manchurian Incident was a Heaven-sent tocsin signalizing at home and abroad the epoch-making dawn of East Asia. Before ... the incident, our public opinion was divided, suffering from domestic trouble and foreign evil. And the successful armament limitation conferences, under the beautiful name of so-called liberalism and national self-determination, merely increased foreign contempt for Japan. But with the extension of the incident, the Japanese people rose to the occasion in the loyal and courageous Yamato spirit and, becoming unified under the August Virtue of His Majesty, marched forward toward the disposal of the incident on the basis of justice (quoted in Tolischus, 1943 252).

The Manchurian Incident and its immediate aftermath also marked a fateful step toward international isolation for Japan. In response to a Chinese appeal, the League of Nations demanded that Japan withdraw its troops from Manchuria by November 1931. When this deadline passed unmet, the League appointed a commission to investigate the situation. Headed by Lord Lytton, the five-man commission was due to arrive in Manchuria in the early months of 1932 to conduct its inquiry. Moving quickly, the Kwantung Army set in motion its plans to establish a new government in Manchuria before the commission arrived. The new Prime Minister Inukai Tsuyoshi had taken up the call for a peaceful settlement to the crisis from former Prime Minister Wakatsuki, whose Cabinet, including Foreign Minister Shidehara, had resigned in December 1931. But a public reeling from the full effects of the economic depression opposed peaceful negotiations and the Kwantung Army moved to establish the new state of Manchukuo with enthusiastic support from the Japanese people.

To head up this supposedly 'independent' state, the Kwantung Army relied on Aishingioro Puyi, the deposed Emperor of China, the last emperor of the Manchu dynasty which had fallen 20 years earlier. Puyi served first as 'President' of the new state, which was formally established on 1 March 1932. In 1934, in an elaborate coronation ceremony, Puyi was enthroned as Emperor of Manchukuo. He 'governed' as a puppet of the Japanese administrators who answered to the Commander-in-Chief of the Kwantung Army. Though Inukai refused to recognize the new state, his successor, Prime Minister Saito Makoto, extended diplomatic recognition to Manchukuo in September 1932. This attempt to build the façade of independence around Manchukuo was timed to take place just before the publication of the Lytton Commission's report.

The October 1932 Lytton Report denounced Japan's actions in Manchuria and denied the Japanese claim that their army was acting in 'self-defense.' Insisting that Manchukuo's 'independence' was not the result of spontaneous action on the part of the local population, the report called on Japan to withdraw all of its forces from Manchuria, with Japanese interests there to be subsequently protected by treaty rights. Faced with the League's acceptance of the report in February 1933, Japan's representative to the League of Nations, Matsuoka Yosuke, grandiosely led his delegation out of the chamber, and Japan withdrew from the League. Save for Germany and Italy, no other nations recognized Manchukuo. The path to the Pacific War was being paved.

By 1934, when the Kwantung Army completed its conquest of Jehol, Manchukuo encompassed four Chinese provinces with a total population of about 30 million. In taking control of Manchuria, Japan vastly expanded its colonial commitment, which now included Taiwan, Korea, and Manchuria. More importantly, the acquisition of Manchuria gave Japan a long shared border with the Soviet Union, which Japan had always eyed with suspicion and mistrust. Thus while Manchuria became a valuable source of raw materials for the development of Japanese heavy industry, it also contributed hugely to Japanese insecurities. From the early 1930s on, the branches of the military argued between themselves over whether China or the Soviet Union posed the main threat to Japan's security and in so doing contributed to Japan's isolation and insecurity.

ULTRA-NATIONALISM

The growing sense of isolation was reinforced by the Japanese peoples' feeling that they had been rejected by the West (as in the Exclusion Act) and had to fight against hostile powers to protect their national interests (as at the League of Nations). In addition, economic despair drove many Japanese to seek escape, either literally, by joining the military, or figuratively, by idealizing Japan's conquests in China. This social and political environment was ripe for the development of extreme nationalist sentiments, which began to take root during the early 1930s. The seeds of the ultra-nationalism of the 1930s had been sown much earlier, argues historian Kenneth B. Pyle (1996: x–xi). Organizations such as the Genyosha, founded in 1881, the Kokuryukai (Amur River Society, also known as the Black Dragon Society), founded in 1901, the Imperial Reservists' Association of 1910, and the Kokuhonsha, founded in 1924, all promoted a belief in Japan's unique character and its 'mission in Asia.'

Indeed, ever since the Meiji Restoration, the government itself had promoted traditional Japanese values as a way to build unity of purpose in the people and encourage the kind of discipline and self-sacrifice necessary to accomplish the goals of rapid industrialization. In 1890, in conjunction with the promulgation of the Meiji Constitution, the Emperor issued the Imperial Rescript on Education, laying out for the Japanese subjects a set of moral, largely Confucian, principles for conduct. The Rescript exhorted them to be filial, harmonious, modest and moral. It called on the Japanese people to 'advance public good and promote common interests; always respect the Constitution and observe the laws; should emergency arise, offer yourselves courageously to the State; and thus guard and maintain the prosperity of Our Imperial Throne coeval with heaven and earth. So shall ye not only be Our good and faithful subjects, but render illustrious the best traditions of your forefathers' (quoted in de Bary, 1958: 646–7). By the 1930s, in the atmosphere of domestic and international crises, the cumulative effect of two generations of young people instructed in the ways of the Imperial Rescript on Education promoted the growth of a rabid and radical form of nationalism.

There was much irony in this. In modernizing and industrializing to preserve itself against Western imperialism, Japan had patterned its reforms and policies on the West. In so doing, even as the government was extolling traditional virtues as a glue to hold the nation together, Japan lost much of its tradition. In both government and society the goal of equality with the West was pursued through Westernization. But to resolve the apparent contradiction between tradition and modernity would be very difficult, if not impossible for many Japanese, for whom the Westernization that swept the nation since the Meiji period felt like a complete rejection of their Japanese identity. Many Japanese felt their past had been obliterated. The nationalism of the 1930s was a reaction to this, an attempt to bring back the traditional pride that had seemingly been sacrificed in the Meiji era rush to modernity. Victory on the battlefield, as in the Sino-Japanese and Russo-Japanese wars that spanned the turn of the century, helped to re-invigorate national pride. In the trying times of the early 1930s, military adventurism again promoted a renewed sense of national pride, and offered a salve to Japan's desperate economic situation.

The extreme racial homogeneity of their nation enabled Japanese nationalists to view Japan as a family state, with the Emperor as 'father.' As one would be loyal to the family, so Japanese nationalists, and ultimately virtually all Japanese, became fanatically loyal to Emperor Hirohito. Japan could boast an unbroken imperial line, an imperial line that traced its descent to the mythical Sun Goddess, Amaterasu. These ideas were promoted by the Meiji leaders as a way to reinforce and solidify the Emperor's position at a time when national unity was considered vital to the very survival of the state. Since the Meiji era, governmental and social leaders had promoted the vague idea of the *kokutai*, that is, the 'national polity,' in effect, the Japanese imperial system of government. *Kokutai* stressed the unique nature of the Japanese state and the close, even organic ties between the people and the Emperor. According to the ideals of *kokutai*, individuals in the state should act like individuals in the family, suppressing their own personalities and offering themselves in service to the state.

By the 1930s, service to the state meant pursuing and promoting Japan's special mission as leader of Asia. This belief that Japan had a unique role in Asia was another cornerstone of the nationalist movement. Prominent nationalist theoretician Okawa Shumei wrote, 'It is my belief that Heaven has chosen Japan as the champion of the East' (quoted in de Bary, 1958: 796). In fact, in the late nineteenth and early twentieth centuries, many in Asia did look to Japan for leadership, as Japan had been the only Asian nation successfully to resist Western imperialism. Young men from China, Vietnam and even Korea flocked to Japan to find the key to its success. But Japan's allure quickly faded when it used its newfound success against the very Asian nations that sought to emulate it. Losing its chance to exert influence in Asia by providing an example of Asian modernity, Japan chose to exert its influence militarily.

Between 1932 and 1936, membership in ultra-nationalist organizations doubled, jumping from 300,000 to 600,000. The backbone of this movement was the lower middle classes, people whom, as Peter Duus (1976: 210) writes, were 'well enough educated to have absorbed the official cult of loyalty to the throne but not well enough educated to doubt its mythical bases.' In general, the grassroots nationalist organizations of the 1930s had little direct impact on actual government policy, but they did provide an all-important base of support for military adventurism, which ultimately helped render the civilian government impotent in the face of military *faits accompli*, like the Manchurian Incident. The primary influence of these groups was to 'anesthetiz[e] public opinion to the dangers of a reckless foreign policy by constantly lauding the superiority of Japanese spirit [and] proclaiming the infallibility of the Imperial Way' (Duus, 1976: 210).

GOVERNMENT REPRESSION

Ideas about the 'infallibility of the Imperial Way' may have moved the spirit of many Japanese during the early 1930s, but the government, bolstered by the regulations of the Peace Preservation Law of 1925, had the authority actually to enforce ultra-nationalist thinking. The law had been invoked in 1928 when the police rounded up thousands of leftists. But one of the first clear examples that this law would be used to enforce intellectual uniformity even among moderate voices came in the spring of 1932. Trampling on the ideal of academic freedom, Education Minister Hatoyama Ichiro, backed by the Cabinet, forced the resignation of Kyoto Imperial University law professor Takigawa Yukitoki for his alleged leftist sympathies. Though the government had earlier targeted communists in academe – Tokyo Imperial University economics professor Morito Tatsuo had been dismissed from his position in 1920 for publishing an article on anarchistic communism – the Takigawa episode revealed that the parameters of acceptable discourse had shrunk dramatically, for though a liberal, Takigawa was not a communist.

The Peace Preservation Law, amended in 1928 when Prime Minister Tanaka insisted that it allow for the death penalty, had by the early 1930s resulted in the imprisonment of some thousands of communists. In the summer of 1933, in a strange intersection of government authority and cultural influence, two jailed leaders of the Japan Communist Party renounced their communist beliefs in public statements issued from their jail cells. Sano Manabu and Nabeyama Sadachika proclaimed their allegiance to the ultra-nationalist ideals of military aggression and the emperor system. This touched off a storm of similar avowals, which fundamentally altered the intellectual climate that would prevail in Japan all the way to the end of the war. The duo's proclamations were not forced by the state, though certainly their incarceration may have had an impact on their decision to repudiate past beliefs. Instead, this wave of *tenko* (about-face) seems to highlight the overwhelming power of the growing ultra-nationalistic orthodoxy. With no political, social, or cultural tradition of democracy and no concept of a 'loyal opposition,' the political landscape of 1930s Japan narrowed. There was no room to disagree. With Japan in economic crisis, and challenged by insecurity on the continent, those who disagreed with the political orthodoxy were considered potential enemies.

The issue of academic freedom was revisited in 1935 when Tokyo Imperial University law professor and Member of the House of Peers Minobe Tatsukichi came under attack for his writings on the 'emperor organ theory.' This theory, which stated that the Emperor was the highest *organ* of the state *under* the constitution, though not the state itself, had been widely accepted in the early part of the twentieth century. By the middle of the 1930s, however, Minobe's espousal of this theory was deemed an attack on the mystical power and authority of the Emperor and his organic connection with his people. Leading the attack on Minobe were ultra-nationalist politicians soon joined by members of the military. Minobe was denounced as a traitor and worse. He was charged with *lèse-majesté* and forced to resign both his seat in the House of Peers and his professorship. His writings were banned and in 1936 he escaped death in two separate assassination attempts. The Minobe case made it clear that the government would not broach any idea that might conceivably run counter to the emperor system. Freedom of thought was fast disappearing.

In order that the Japanese people might know exactly what thought was expected of them, in March 1937 the government published *Kokutai no hongi* (*Fundamentals of Our National Polity*). Relying on ancient Japanese classics, the *Kokutai no hongi* spelled out the principles of Japan's Emperor system, stating clearly the emperor was the supreme and inviolate authority in the *kazoku kokka*, the family state. The document also upheld militaristic ideas about Japan's unique mission in Asia. As the official orthodoxy of the state, *Kokutai no hongi* became the principal ethics text in the schools. In the family state, individualism was derided as a selfish and corrupt idea; uniformity of spirit was lauded. The official endorsement of *Kokutai no hongi*, coupled with governmental repression and the sense that Japan was being pressured internationally from all sides, meant that throughout the war years dissent was virtually non-existent.

THE 'SHOWA RESTORATION'

The most serious and most influential ultra-nationalists served in the military, where they had the power to act on their beliefs. One key figure in the philosophical development of Japanese ultra-nationalism was Kita Ikki (1884–1937), whose ideas had a huge impact in military circles. Originally a socialist, Kita stressed Japan's mission as liberator of Asia. To prepare Japan for its rightful role as leader of Asia, Kita advocated a return to direct imperial rule. This would be achieved via a violent *coup d'état* that would suspend the Constitution, impose martial law, and eliminate the corrupt politicians and bureaucrats who stood in the way of the Emperor's direct relationship with his people. Sounding the alarm, Kita wrote his most influential piece, *Nihon kaizo hoan taiko* (*An Outline Plan for the Reorganization of Japan*) in 1923: 'At present the Japanese empire is faced with a national crisis unparalleled in its history ... the fundamental doctrine of the emperor as representative of the people and as pillar of the nation must be made clear' (quoted in de Bary, 1958: 775–8).

Armed with Kita's admonitions to effect a 'purification of the imperial court', young members of the military embarked on assassination sprees aimed at clearing away corruption around the throne and effecting a 'Showa Restoration.'[1] The first attempt to put their ideas into action was the March Incident of 1931, six months before the decisive Manchurian Incident. The chief planners of the incident were members of the Sakurakai, or Cherry Blossom Society. This group, founded in the autumn of 1930 and consisting primarily of Army general staff officers, was strongly influenced by Kita Ikki and nationalist ideologue Okawa Shumei. They took as their icon the cherry blossom, long associated with the samurai warrior, which 'bursts into being and then suddenly, when the time has come, falls in an instant to the ground in clean and beautiful death' (Butow, 1961: 33). The group, which strongly advocated an aggressive policy toward Manchuria, was led by Lieutenant-Colonel Hashimoto Kingoro.

The Sakurakai set 20 March for the coup attempt. Working with General Koiso Kuniaki, then Chief of the Military Affairs Bureau, the conspirators planned to arm a group of civilians who would stage demonstrations outside the Diet Building. In the ensuing chaos, the conspirators would fan out and commit their acts of violence against politicians, including the Prime Minister, and install War Minister General Ugaki Kazushige as head of a military government. When Ugaki withdrew his initial support, however, the plot fell apart.

But plans for a similar plot were revived again in October, just a month after the Manchurian Incident. Once again, Hashimoto, Okawa and other members of the Sakurakai aimed for a 'thorough purging of the ideological and political atmosphere through the wholesale assassination of the ministers of the cabinet' (Butow, 1961: 51). The civilian government was to be replaced with a military one headed by General Araki Sadao. Once again the conspiracy fell through when Araki refused to cooperate. The conspirators were arrested in mid-October, but in what would become a dangerous pattern, they were not punished because they had acted 'sincerely' (though wrong-headedly) in the interests of the empire.

These opening salvos of the 'Showa Restoration,' though unsuccessful in achieving their direct goals, furthered the aims of the Kwantung Army by intimidating the civilian government into condoning the Army's moves in Manchuria. In the aftermath of the failed October Incident, yet another group of conspirators arose to carry out the aims of the October conspirators. This was the Ketsumeidan, or 'Blood League.' Mostly young peasants, the members of this group were not only concerned with Japan's international security, but with the economic misery in the countryside. Working in concert with both naval officers and army cadets, the conspirators planned a day of violence that would destroy the existing government and result in the declaration of martial law. On the afternoon of Sunday, 15 May 1932, a small group of conspirators broke into Prime Minister Inukai's residence, determined to kill him in retaliation for his initial resistance to the Army's goals in the Manchurian Incident. His attempts to engage them in a discussion failed and he was shot to death. Simultaneously, other conspirators lobbed bombs at the residence of Makino Nobuaki, the Lord Keeper of the Privy Seal, and at the Mitsubishi Bank and the Bank of Japan (these financial organizations, they believed, helped prop up the corrupt civilian government). Power and police stations provided other targets for the ruthless conspirators.

Once again the conspiracy failed to achieve its stated end. Yet the 15 May Incident dealt a fatal blow to the ever-weakening political parties and proved a decisive political turning point for Japan. Inukai was replaced as Prime Minister by Saito Makoto, a retired admiral who, acting on the advice of the last surviving Meiji era leader, Prince Saionji Kinmochi, appointed a 'cabinet of national unity' in a bid to restore national order. The cabinet consisted of representatives from the nearly defunct political parties, the bureaucracy, and the military. It was this cabinet that formally recognized Manchukuo, thus endorsing the Army insubordination that had resulted in the establishment of Japan's puppet state in Manchuria. The precedent was set, and from this point on, open disagreement with the military was virtually non-existent.

In another sign of the times, War Minister Araki Sadao publicly praised the 15 May conspirators as 'pure and naïve young men ... [who] performed [their actions] in the sincere belief that they were for the benefit of Imperial Japan' (quoted in Duus, 1976: 211). Their trial was a heated affair that attracted national attention. Sympathy went not to the murder victims but to the conspirators, who were widely regarded as heroes. Most received light sentences, and even the stiffest sentence of hard labor for life was eventually, like the rest, reduced; some sentences were eliminated altogether.

These early events in the 'Showa Restoration' served to sharpen the growing split between two rival factions within the military. Since the early 1930s, army members, especially the young officer corps, had begun to coalesce into two rather loosely grouped factions. These were the Kodo or 'Imperial Way' faction, and the Tosei, or 'Control' faction. The Kodo faction, led by Generals Araki and Mazaki Jinzaburo, believed in direct, violent action to clear away the corruption around the throne and establish direct imperial rule. This group, whose supporters were primarily from the ranks of field grade officers, put great store in the fighting spirit that they believed the Japanese soldiers possessed as a birthright from their samurai forbears. The fighting spirit of the Japanese infantry, they maintained, would prevail even over superior technology. The primary threat to Japan's security, they believed, would be the Soviet Union.

The Tosei faction was led by Ishiwara Kanji and Tojo Hideki and drew its primary support from within the War Ministry. The Tosei faction believed that the Kodo faction's violent efforts to restore direct imperial rule were ill-considered and would only result in obstructing the nation's real need, which was mobilizing both technologically and economically for total war, which they believed would be fought against China.

By the middle of 1935 the violent tactics of the Showa Restoration were for the first time used not against civilian opponents, but against perceived enemies in the ranks of the military itself. On 12 August 1935 the rivalry between the Kodo and Tosei factions erupted in violence when Lieutenant-Colonel Aizawa Saburo entered the office of Major-General Nagata Tetsuzan and assassinated him by plunging a sword through his body. Nagata, appointed Chief of the Military Affairs Bureau in early 1934, was viewed by many as 'the most brilliant officer in the army,' and had been a leading member of the Tosei faction (Hane, 1996: 264). Aizawa, a fanatical member of the Kodo faction, blamed Nagata for forcing the resignation of Kodo faction leader Mazaki Jinzaburo from his position as inspector of military education. The aftermath of the Manchurian Incident revealed that the civilian government had little control over the military. Now, the Aizawa Incident called into question whether the military could control its own ranks. The Showa Restoration was being unleashed within the military itself.

The conflict within the Army would play itself out in the climactic act of the Showa Restoration, the 26 February Incident in 1936. In the early morning hours, 1,400 troops from three Army regiments surrounded the Imperial Palace, cordoned off downtown Tokyo, took over governmental offices and went on an assassination spree that left three government leaders dead and others wounded. Led by young officers of the Kodo faction, the group declared martial law, and announced its purpose:

> It is clearer than light that our country is on the verge of war with Russia, China, Britain and America, who wish to crush our ancestral land. Unless we now rise and annihilate the unrighteous and disloyal creatures who surround the Imperial Throne and obstruct the course of true reform, the Imperial Prestige will fall to the ground ... We are persuaded that it is our duty to remove the villains who surround the Throne (quoted in Butow, 1961: 64).

For two days the insurgents met little resistance and held their ground, convinced that others in the Army, as well as members of the Navy, would join them in common cause. Finally, on 28 February, military authorities, led primarily by Ishiwara Kanji, a conspirator in the Manchurian Incident who was horrified by the breakdown of Army discipline, began to refer to the leaders as 'rebels' and moved to defuse the situation. The Navy, too, joined ranks against the rebels, moving its ships into Tokyo Bay and training its guns on them. But most important was the fact that Emperor Hirohito himself repudiated the rebels, who, after all, claimed to be acting in his interest. When the Emperor disavowed their actions, and his order was conveyed to the insurgents, they finally dispersed. The troops went home and the leaders were arrested and put on trial. Some 124 were tried, and 103 were sentenced. Of these, fifteen were executed, including Kita Ikki, who, though not a direct participant, was considered the philosophical father of the plot.

The Showa Restoration had failed. But the violence that colored domestic political affairs since the early 1930s nevertheless had a strong impact on Japan, one that would have significant effects in the next decade. Ironically, rather than weakening the power of the military, the failure of the 26 February military insurgency strengthened it. The Army used the aftermath of the 26 February Incident to purge Kodo fanatics from its ranks. The Tosei faction was now ascendant. To make sure that purged generals of the Kodo faction were excluded from serving in the Cabinet, the Army reintroduced the regulation, abandoned in 1913, that the War Minister must be on active service, so once again the military enjoyed veto power over the Cabinet. As Japan moved ever closer to war with China, the Tosei-dominated military would increasingly call the shots.

NOTES

1   Showa was the imperial reign title of Emperor Hirohito, and the Showa period lasted from 1926 to 1989. The term 'Showa Restoration' harked back to the Meiji Restoration of 1868.

CHAPTER FIVE

THE ROAD TO WAR

The military's voice in politics had grown louder and louder during the first half of the 1930s. Though the attempts by radicals within the military to effect a 'Showa Restoration' had failed to revive direct imperial rule, the series of coup attempts and assassinations of the early 1930s intimidated the civilian government into accepting the military's dominant policy-making role. The purges carried out in the aftermath of the 26 February Incident left the Army more unified and cohesive, but power was still wielded by an array of competing interests, including the weak but lasting political parties, industrialists, and the bureaucracy. Since all were, like the population as a whole, strong adherents of the virulent nationalism that metastasized throughout society in the early 1930s, military adventurism was accepted and promoted as vital to Japan's national interests. Rejecting any criticism of its foreign policy from the international community as racist and obstructionist, Japan isolated itself from its former allies.

In midsummer 1937, the Japanese government found itself at a critical turning point when hostilities broke out between Chinese and Japanese troops stationed near Beijing. The decision to expand this unintended clash proved a tragic step that inexorably drew Japan deeper and deeper into conflict not only in China, but with the nations of the West. Indeed, by the early 1940s, former allies had become enemies, obstacles to Japan's 'historic mission' to oust the lingering Western presence in Asia and carve out an autarkic empire there. By the end of 1941, Japan hovered on the very brink of war with its most dangerous opponent: the United States.

WAR WITH CHINA

China had steadfastly refused to extend diplomatic recognition to Japan's puppet state of Manchukuo. In 1933, shortly after the creation of Man-chukuo, the Kwantung Army sought to extend a buffer zone into northern China. With a series of military engagements the Kwantung Army intimi-dated Nationalist leader Chiang Kaishek, always more concerned about the growing Chinese Communist menace than with the Japanese, into signing the Tangku Truce in April 1933. This agreement allowed Japan to station troops beyond Manchukuo, as far south as the Great Wall, and to establish a demilitarized zone in eastern Hebei province, which included Beijing and the important seaport Tianjin. Suspicious of Japanese motives since the 1915 Twenty-One Demands, the Chinese renewed their anti-Japanese activities. When anti-Japanese demonstrations erupted in Tianjin in May 1935, the Kwantung Army and the Japanese Tianjin garrison moved to stop them. The Japanese aim, as formulated by officers in the field, was to oust all Nationalist troops from northern China and turn the area into an autonomous region.

In Tokyo, the fall-out of the 26 February Incident toppled the Cabinet of Okada Keisuke. He was replaced by his Foreign Minister, Hirota Koki, who became Prime Minister in March 1936. Hirota had strong connections to the Tosei faction in the army, and was a long-time member of the Genyosha, one of the earliest ultra-nationalist societies. Presiding over the political situation in the shaky aftermath of the 26 February Incident, Hirota dealt with Army demands for the reintroduction of the requirement that the Ministers of War and of the Navy be appointed from the ranks of officers on active service. This requirement had been eliminated in the more democratic era of 1912 in the wake of the Taisho political crisis, when the population, angered by the Army's role in collapsing the second Saionji Cabinet, had demanded that this military prerogative be removed in the interests of 'constitutional government.' By allowing the reintroduction of the requirement, Hirota was in effect capitulating to the military, and the military's role in political life once again racheted up. Now the Army and Navy had control over the formation of the Cabinet: if the Army felt sure that the newly appointed Cabinet would be favorable to their concerns, they could go ahead and appoint a minister to complete the Cabinet. If they felt the proposed Cabinet was not in tune with their ideas, they could refuse to appoint a minister and the Cabinet would be unable to function. The officer serving as Minister of War or Minister of the Navy would not only feel a sense of obligation to those who ensured his appointment, but would actually be subject to the orders of their military superiors.

As Foreign Minister, Hirota had tried to improve Sino-Japanese relations. His efforts, however, were basically aimed at paving the way for a more solid Japanese presence in China. Hirota believed that Japan's most serious security challenge came not from China, but from the Soviet Union. If the Soviet Union was the primary threat, then Japan could not afford to have trouble at its rear. To buttress Japan against this security threat, Hirota concluded an Anti-Comintern Pact with Germany in November 1936. The Pact committed the two nations to exchanging information about the Comintern and to work to limit its effect. However, a secret protocol of the Pact stipulated that in the event of a Soviet attack on either nation, the other would assist by refraining from any actions that might be helpful to the Soviets. While this was a step away from the international isolation into which Japan had withdrawn when Matsuoka stormed out of the League of Nations in 1933, it signified Japan was casting its lot with the most combative of allies, Nazi Germany, and alienating itself ever further from Great Britain and the United States. Moreover, in signing the agreement, Japan incurred the mistrust and hostility of the Soviet Union.

China's refusal to recognize Manchukuo was troublesome for the new Cabinet, which, in October 1935, adopted Hirota's Three Principles as policy toward China. The Three Principles called on China to suppress anti-Japanese and Chinese Communist activity and to offer a *de facto* recognition of Manchukuo that would enable Japan to access trading rights in northern China. Characteristically, this policy was not aggressive enough for Army officers in the field who wanted it stipulated that reunification of China under Nationalist control was both 'unnecessary and undesirable' (Hane, 1992: 274). Following the pattern established in the Manchurian Incident, officers of the Kwantung Army pursued more aggressive policies in the field than authorized by the government in Tokyo. Throughout the last half of 1935, the Kwantung Army kept up a steady pressure in northern China, launching a series of military maneuvers designed to extend the demilitarized zone outlined in the Tangku Truce to include all of Hebei province. If the Soviet Union was the main threat to Japan's presence in Manchuria, it was of vital importance that the rear be secure.

Meanwhile, the Young Marshal, Zhang Xueliang, had joined ranks with Chiang Kaishek and was following his orders to exterminate the Communists in northern China, which, after 1935, had become an important center of power for the Chinese Communist Party (CCP). In the mid-1920s, the Communists had been Chiang's allies in a united front designed to reunify warlord-fragmented China; then Chiang brutally turned his Nationalist forces on them, forcing them to flee to the mountainous country of southeastern China. In this poverty-stricken area, the CCP built up a series of bases, but were constantly threatened by Chiang's extermination campaigns. In 1934, Chiang launched his fifth campaign against the Communists, forcing them to embark on the Long March, which after a year of hardship brought them to the north. There they set to rebuilding their decimated party, attracting members in part by representing themselves as the strongest anti-Japanese force in China. Chiang Kaishek was loathe to use his resources against the Japanese: the Japanese, said Chiang, are a disease of the skin; the Communists are a disease of the heart. His strategy was to eliminate the Communists first; then, from a position of strength, he would turn his attention to the Japanese.

This strategy was deeply troubling for many Chinese, not least the

Young Marshal Zhang Xueliang himself, whose father had been murdered by the Japanese in 1928. By early 1936, Zhang had secretly consulted with the Communists about their shared belief that another Nationalist–Communist united front was necessary to eliminate the Japanese presence in northern China. From his base in Nanjing (Nanking) in southern China, Chiang Kaishek was insulated against the rabid anti-Japanese sentiments developing in the north, where the Japanese threat was immediate. Aware that his commanders in the north were expressing reservations about his continued insistence on fighting the Communists, in December 1936 Chiang traveled north to Xian to meet with his generals, including Zhang Xueliang, and to launch a renewed offensive against the Communists.

In a series of difficult and heated discussions with Zhang, Chiang remained adamant that his forces must be used first against the Communists. Zhang finally resorted to force, and in the early morning hours of 12 December 1936 he ordered his men to surround the compound where Chiang slept. Awakened by the sound of gunshots, Chiang crawled out of a window of his bedroom and escaped up the hill at the back of the compound. Still in his pajamas, Chiang was apprehended and taken into custody. After two weeks of protracted negotiations, with Zhou Enlai serving as chief negotiator for the Communists, Chiang was released on Christmas Day, and the 'Xian Incident' was over. Chiang had at last agreed to enter into a united front with the Communists against the Japanese.

The hero's welcome Chiang received upon his return to Nanjing, from a population elated that their resources would finally be turned against the foreign invaders, made it clear to the Japanese that China possessed a new resolve. It was in the midst of this revival of Chinese nationalism in midsummer 1937 that the 'China Incident' broke out, as China and Japan faced each other in a fateful challenge. Since the beginning of the summer, Japanese troops had been conducting maneuvers near the Marco Polo Bridge, just outside Beijing.[1] On the night of 7 July 1937 the Japanese were firing blank cartridges into the air, as they had been authorized to do by the Chinese, when Chinese troops fired into the area. Though no one was hit, when the exercise was over, one Japanese soldier 'turned up missing.' In retaliation, the Japanese commander ordered his troops to attack the Chinese. Over the next couple of days, fighting and negotiations continued concurrently. By 9 July, the missing soldier was found and the local commanders arranged a cease-fire.

Within the Army disagreement existed over whether or not to use the skirmish as a pretext for settling the China problem once and for all by carving out a separate Japanese-controlled state in northern China. General Ishiwara Kanji, though associated with the Tosei faction which advocated preparation for war with China, was one among several high-ranking figures in the Army who thought that war with China at the time was ill-advised and would make Japan even more vulnerable to the Soviet Union. On 11 July the new Prime Minister Prince Konoe announced his Cabinet's decision that Japanese troops in northern China would be reinforced with five additional divisions. In the event of significant progress in negotiations with the Chinese, he would cancel this order. Konoe declared that the situation warranted a local settlement and a policy of 'non-enlargement' (Hane, 1992: 275). Yet at the same time he issued a public statement declaring the problem was 'entirely the result of an anti-Japanese military action on the part of the Chinese.' 'The Chinese authorities,' he said, 'must apologize to us for the illegal anti-Japanese actions' (quoted in Crowley, 1966: 331).

With the memory of the Xian Incident fresh in his memory, Chiang Kaishek realized he could not afford even the appearance of being soft on the Japanese. Anxious to prove his new resolve, he announced: 'If we allow one more inch of our territory to be lost, we shall be guilty of an unpardonable crime against our race' (quoted in Crowley, 1966: 335). By the end of July, fighting broke out between Japanese and Chinese troops in the area around Beijing, and Chiang sent four divisions to northern China as reinforcements. On 13 August, in a huge and unsuccessful gamble, Chiang sent Chinese bombers to attack the Japanese settlement in Shanghai. Konoe's government responded by authorizing the dispatch of two army divisions to Shanghai. The Sino-Japanese conflict had spilled into the south and by 17 August the Japanese Cabinet officially decided to abandon the localization policy and instead prepare for general war. 'Japan,' declared Prime Minister Konoe, had been 'forced to resort to resolute action to bring sense to the Nanjing government by punishing the atrocious Chinese army' (quoted in Crowley, 1966: 343). Though not planned by the government, nor strongly supported by the likes of Ishiwara Kanji and other members of the Army General Staff, Japan's eight-year war in China had just begun.

In the early months of the war, the Japanese public met Japan's easy success with wild enthusiasm. Fifteen new Japanese divisions arrived in north and central China imposing stunning loses on Chiang. In the fall of 1937, Chiang's forces suffered 250,000 casualties to Japan's 40,000 casualties (Spence, 1990: 447). As they drove toward Chiang's capital at Nanjing, field commanders predicted that China would be completely defeated within six months (Duus, 1976: 216).

By early December, Japanese forces launched an offensive against Nanjing, capturing the city on 13 December. Completely routed, Chiang's military retreated, eventually establishing a wartime capital a thousand miles up the Yangzi (Yangtze) River at Chongqing (Chungking). In the six weeks that followed the capture of Nanjing, Japanese soldiers, with the consent of their commanders, unleashed a horrifying riot of death and destruction on the defenseless civilian population of the city. In an investigation conducted after the war, the International Military Tribunal for the Far East estimated that Japanese soldiers killed over 260,000 civilians during this 'Rape of Nanking.' Some historians have put the figure at over 350,000 (Chang, 1997: 4). Men, women and children were killed, raped and tortured with methods whose cruelty defies imagination.

One month later, in January 1938, Konoe entered into negotiations with Chiang, demanding that China recognize Manchukuo and create a demilitarized zone in northern China that would provide a buffer for their Manchurian puppet state. Chiang rejected the proposal. Konoe's response was to declare that Japan would no longer recognize Chiang's government in China. In doing so he ignored the reservations of the Army General Staff, who, exercising a bit more caution than the belligerent younger field grade officers of the Kwantung Army, believed that despite Japan's early victories, war with China would prove a dangerous drain on Japan's resources. Negotiations were no longer an option. China had, in Konoe's words, 'blindly persist[ed] in its opposition to Japan, with no consideration either internally for the Chinese people in their miserable plight or externally for the peace and tranquillity of all Asia.' Therefore, he continued:

> the Japanese government will cease henceforth to deal with that government and it looks forward to the establishment and growth of a new Chinese regime ... With this regime, the Japanese government will cooperate fully for the adjustment of Sino-Japanese relations and the building of a rejuvenated China. (quoted in Crowley, 1966: 375–6)

Japan thus committed itself to establishing new regimes in China, and to the disastrous policy of a 'war of annihilation' against Chiang Kaishek's Nationalist government.

Konoe's fateful pledge propelled Japan down the path to a war it could not win. Although the government in Tokyo had never planned to establish a colony in Manchuria, the defense of Japan's puppet state there had become axiomatic. Now, six years later, Japan was at war with China. Once again Japan found itself engaged in an unplanned war, but one deemed necessary to the very survival of Japan in the face of a hostile world. It was, writes historian Kenneth B. Pyle (1996: 201), a decision that 'tragically underrated the difficulties involved.' In the years to come, Japan would allocate huge resources to the effort to subdue China, increasing its sense of insecurity on other fronts. Also, the war with China would lead to the imposition of ever tighter controls on the domestic population. Perhaps most importantly, the 'China problem' would become the major sticking point in relations between Japan and the United States.

The man who led Japan to this fateful decision was Prime Minister Prince Konoe Fumimaro (1891–1945).[2] A member of the court nobility, Konoe was widely respected by civilian and military leaders as well as the

Emperor. Because of this, he was asked to serve as Prime Minister in the unsettled year after the 26 February Incident. Konoe was a native of Tokyo and had been educated at Kyoto Imperial University. He was a protégé of Saionji Kinmochi, who, from 1924 until his death in 1940, had immense status as the last surviving leader from the Meiji Restoration era. Konoe's sophisticated and urbane demeanor belied a wavering, indecisive character. Though viewed by foreign leaders as a moderate, it was under his leadership that Japan went to war with China, and later would make the decision to attack the United States at Pearl Harbor. He was, wrote former Foreign Minister Shigemitsu Mamoru (1958: 134), 'esteemed by all classes, high and low. Surely such a man was not cast to be the puppet of the militarists; he himself at all events did not think it. And yet that is just the grave responsibility he must bear. He did in fact become the puppet of the Army.'

On 11 November 1938, with the war in China just over one year old, Konoe announced his vision of a 'New Order in East Asia.' This 'New Order' would link all of East Asia under Japanese leadership, creating a self-sufficient economic bloc free from Western domination. The fight in Asia, argued ultra-nationalist theoretician Okawa Shumei, would be 'a struggle between the great powers of the East and the West which will decide their existence … there will be one country acting as the champion of Asia' (quoted in de Bary, 1958: 795). That country, of course, would be Japan. Announcing the New Order in East Asia, Konoe sympathized with China, which had been, he said, 'the victim of the imperialistic ambitions and rivalries of the Occidental Powers.' Establishing a New Order in East Asia was Japan's historic mission in Asia, a mission that held all the urgency of a holy war. 'Japan,' Konoe said, was 'eager to see a new order in East Asia – a new structure based on true justice' (quoted in Crowley, 1970: 255). But as historian Peter Duus (1976: 190) has pointed out, Japan was merely cloaking its imperialism in the garb of anti-colonialism, a fallacious proposition. In truth, Japan simply sought to establish its own hegemony over Asia. Eventually this would take shape as the Greater East Asian Co-Prosperity Sphere, an economically self-sufficient Asia led by Japan that would encompass Manchukuo, Korea, Taiwan, huge swathes of China, and before the war was over, former European colonies in Southeast Asia and the South Pacific.

Konoe's bitterness about the effects of Western imperialism in Asia highlights some important elements in the genesis of Japan's 'mission in Asia.' It was Western imperialism, in the form of Commodore Perry's arrival in Japan in 1853, that prompted the Meiji Restoration of 1868. The drive to free itself from the unequal treaties imposed on it by the Western nations had compelled Japan to embark on the series of reforms designed to modernize and industrialize the nation. In the process, Japan 'lost' its illustrious past.

By the turn of the century, Japan had strengthened itself enough to wage war first against China, then against Russia. When World War I broke out, Japan sided with the Allied powers and pressed for concessions from China in the Twenty-One Demands of 1915. At the Paris Peace Conference that followed World War I, US President Woodrow Wilson outlined the framework of the postwar era in his famous 'Fourteen Points' that spelled out the rights of national self-determination. In the post-World War I era, the West repudiated colonialism; although the Western nations did not rush to relinquish their colonial possessions, neither did they add to them. Konoe, who had attended the conference in 1919, criticized the resulting treaties as nothing more than the West's attempt to preserve the status quo. After World War I, Japan was, for the first time, militarily and economically able to pursue expansion. Since the Meiji Restoration, Japan had modeled itself on the West, and the way the Western nations expressed national strength was by taking on colonies. But suddenly, when Japan began to pursue expansionist policies in Asia, it seemed the rules had changed and Japan became the object of Western criticism. Thus Japan viewed the West's criticism of Japan's expansion in Asia as self-serving hypocrisy, designed merely to obstruct Japan, to keep it small and weak, and to protect the West's global hegemony.

The United States at first responded warily to Japanese actions in China. President Roosevelt condemned Japan's aggression in his October 1937 'quarantine' speech: 'When an epidemic of physical disease starts to spread, the community approves and joins in a quarantine of the patients in order to protect the health of the community' (quoted in Toland, 1970: 58–9). Others, including Secretary of State Cordell Hull and Ambassador to Japan Joseph Grew, were not so quick to come to China's side against Japan. As hostilities continued, however, American criticism grew, and by the summer of 1938 the United States placed an embargo on war *matériel* to Japan. At the same time, a border clash broke out on the Manchukuo–Soviet border. Japanese Army officers in the area, who had argued passionately that Japan should be preserving its resources for war against the Soviets, hoped to use the dispute to deliver serious damage to the Soviet forces. The Soviets, however, were militarily much superior to the Japanese, and the Japanese were forced to reach a settlement. Japan's actions in China were causing increasing friction in their international relations.

Moreover, a quick Japanese victory in China had not materialized. Konoe, always the reluctant Prime Minister, resigned his post in January 1939. The premiership passed to Baron Hiranuma Kiichiro (1867–1952), a prominent right-wing politician and head of the ultra-nationalist Koku-honsha. Hiranuma's Cabinet, anxious to shore up its defenses against the Soviet Union, continued the debate, begun during Konoe's tenure, over entering into an alliance with Nazi Germany. Germany had recognized

Manchukuo in 1933, and in 1936 Japan and Germany had signed the Anti-Comintern Pact. After the outbreak of Japan's war with China, Hitler had withdrawn German military advisers from China. Both shared a serious concern about the Soviet Union. These issues brought Germany and Japan closer together, and, in the process, increased Japan's alienation from Great Britain and the United States. So when in August 1939 Germany signed a non-aggression pact with the Soviet Union, Japan was stunned and the Hiranuma Cabinet discredited. Hiranuma, pronouncing the situation 'queer and complicated' (quoted in Shigemitsu, 1958: 171), resigned and once again the premiership changed hands, now passing to General Abe Nobuyuki (1875–1953).

Abe took office on 30 August 1939. The very next day, Hitler's armies launched their attack on Poland. In Japan, news of the Nazi blitzkrieg was met with euphoria. The new Cabinet declined to declare Japan's neutrality in the conflict; for Japan, the war in Europe would open new opportunities and new riches. But as inflation ballooned in Japan, Abe's premiership crumbled in January 1940, another in a string of short-lived cabinets that highlighted Japan's political instability.

Abe was replaced by Admiral Yonai Mitsumasa, who personally was strongly opposed to an alliance with Germany. Rather than promoting war with Britain and the United States, Yonai favored cooperating with the Anglo-American powers. Shortly after Yonai's appointment, the Diet witnessed the first – and last – public indictment of Japan's China policy when Diet member Saito Takao remarked to the assembly that Japan's pursuit of a New Order in East Asia 'may, in fact, be detrimental to the future of our nation. [T]he government,' he declared, 'was using the beautiful sounding notion of a sacred war in vain; and, disregarding the national sacrifices involved, it is constantly harping on the notion of international justice, moral diplomacy, and co-existence and co-prosperity' (quoted in Crowley, 1970: 256–7). Saito's remarks were immediately criticized as treasonous. By equating Japan's mission in Asia as 'substantively the same as wars waged by Caucasians,' the administration declared, Saito was undermining the morale and the mission of the Japanese people. He was forced out of the Diet, and domestic criticism of Japan's policy in China was silenced.

Germany's advances in Europe coincided with a new development in China that seemed to augur well for Japan. In March 1940, Wang Jingwei (Wang Chingwei), once Chiang Kaishek's second-in-command, announced his decision to cooperate with Japan. Believing that China could not win a war against Japan and fearful of the rising Communist influence, Wang agreed to serve as president of Japan's new puppet regime in China.

Wang's defection was not followed with similar defections from other Nationalist Chinese officials, as the Japanese hoped. Nevertheless, these promising developments in Europe and China strengthened the hand of

Army officers who despised Prime Minister Yonai's friendly posture toward the United States and Great Britain and were infuriated by his refusal to entertain an alliance with Germany. In July 1940, War Minister Hata Shunroku resigned from the Cabinet. The Army refused to appoint a successor, thus forcing the collapse of the Yonai Cabinet.

After some resistance, Prince Konoe agreed to form another Cabinet, inaugurated on 22 July 1940. Konoe's reputation as a moderate made him the choice of those who would curb the rash impulses of the extremists, but once again, as with the outbreak of war with China in 1937, the second Konoe Cabinet would lead Japan into war with the United States.

Shortly after having taken office, Konoe convened a meeting with his new War Minister, Tojo Hideki, his new Foreign Minister, Matsuoka Yosuke, and his Navy Minister, Yoshida Zengo, to outline the country's basic foreign policy. The decisions that resulted from this meeting, compiled in a report titled 'The Main Principles of Basic National Policy,' were formally approved by the Cabinet as a whole on 26 July. This document provided a detailed blueprint for achieving Japan's goals in Asia. The first order of business was to bring the war in China to a successful conclusion that would in turn enable Japan to establish the economically self-sufficient New Order in East Asia that Konoe had envisioned since 1938. This called for military build-up, and thoroughgoing reforms in Japan's political, economic, and educational policy as well. In short, the 'Policy' attempted to focus all of Japan's resources, economic and human, on war.

A liaison conference on 27 July, between the Cabinet and the Army and Navy Chiefs of Staff further clarified Japan's foreign policy goals in light of the changing situation in Europe, and spelled out Japan's intention of moving into Southeast Asia. Hitler's successes in Europe had opened opportunities for Japan. Though the Soviet Union remained a concern, a southern advance now seemed especially promising. Responding to these changes in the international situation, the conference mapped out an approach for solving Japan's 'problems' in the south. A favorable resolution of the China situation remained the top priority, but, the Cabinet outlined, Japan should not put all other goals on hold. So 'The Main Principles of Japan's Policy for Coping with the Situation in Accordance with World Developments' spelled out contingency plans for Japan in the event that a favorable resolution in China was not forthcoming. Japan, the Policy said, should be ready to use force to pursue opportunities to the south. In doing so, Japan should try to confine its conflicts to Great Britain, but recognizing that this might also cause friction with the United States, Japan should also militarily prepare itself for the possibility of war with the United States. Thus, in a series of decisions made shortly after taking office for the second time, Konoe committed the country not only to a continuation of fighting in China, but also to the prospect of expanding hostilities against new enemies.

Some of the groundwork for this policy had been laid in late June 1940, shortly before the fall of the Yonai Cabinet. The outbreak of war in Europe, while providing new opportunities for Japan, also vastly increased Japan's economic dependence on the United States. Thus Japan became concerned about securing access to Southeast Asian resources. As a first step in this direction, Japan demanded that France, just defeated by German armies, allow Japan to blockade China's southern border with Indochina and also demanded that the Dutch guarantee Japan a million tons of oil from the Dutch East Indies. This was Japan's first overt move south, and it put the United States on alert. The United States responded in July 1940, by expanding the 1938 embargo on war *matériel* to include scrap iron and steel. The Japanese, unable to fathom the US position, concluded that American efforts to hamper their goals in Asia were simply another example of arrogant American racism.

Soon after the Cabinet decided on the southern advance policy at the liaison conference of 27 July, Japan pressed its advantage in French Indochina. At the same time, to bolster Japan's position in the south, Konoe's Foreign Minister Matsuoka Yosuke resurrected the issue of a treaty with Nazi Germany. A volatile character, Matsuoka had served as director of the South Manchurian Railroad and strongly supported Japan's aggressive stance in China. British Ambassador to Japan Sir Robert Craigie described Matsuoka as 'a stubborn and determined man with an acute mind,' but he was also rash and impulsive. Matsuoka was talkative and flamboyant, saddled with nicknames like 'Mr 50,000 Words,' and 'Talking Machine.' A graduate of the University of Oregon who spoke fluent English, Matsuoka, with his flair for the dramatic, had led the Japanese delegation storming out of the League of Nations after that body had censured Japan's actions in Manchuria (Toland, 1970: 77).

By 22 September 1940, Matsuoka succeeded in forcing Vichy France into an agreement allowing Japan to maintain air bases in Tonkin, in northern Indochina, and to garrison troops there. The agreement, concluded in Hanoi, also allowed Japan to use the area to transport troops and supplies into China. In return, France was guaranteed continued sovereignty over the province. In effect, Japan extracted what it wanted, while the French continued to administer the province, a very sweet deal for Japan.

Matsuoka proposed further shoring up Japan's presence in Southeast Asia by means of a pact with Germany and Italy. Such a pact, Matsuoka argued, would not provoke American anger as the Navy feared; instead it would function as the most important restraint on the United States, enabling Japan to continue its southern advance without American interference. Moreover, he argued, because Germany and the Soviet Union were already linked by their non-aggression treaty, a pact with Germany would help smooth relations between Japan and the Soviets. The Cabinet, the Army and Navy all gave Matsuoka the go-ahead, and the Tripartite Pact was signed in Berlin on 27 September 1940.[3] The main gist of the Pact stipulated that 'when and if any of the signatories were attacked by any third power not then engaged in the European War or the China Incident, the other two would aid her with all political, economic, or military means.' Additionally, the Pact stated that the signatories' relations with the Soviet Union were not to be affected (Hane, 1992: 293). Clearly, the Pact was aimed at the United States.

TIGHTENING CONTROL

Soon after concluding this pact, the Konoe Cabinet made a move to quiet the political squabbling between the political parties, the Army, the Navy, the Diet and industrialists that had characterized Japanese policy-making since the start of the war with China in 1937. Though wider in scope, the effort was similar in intent to the 'cabinets of national unity' that followed the 1932 15 May Incident; the result was the creation a single, unified political body called the Imperial Rule Assistance Association (IRAA) in October 1940. In preparation for this new political entity, the political parties voluntarily dissolved themselves, bringing to a conclusion the party decline begun in 1932. Though originally sponsored by Konoe, the IRAA was primarily the bailiwick of the Army. Enveloping their aims in vague nationalistic rhetoric that was characteristic of the era, the Army described the IRAA as an organization that would allow 'leaders and people [to be] coupled together, working smoothly in unison' (Shigemitsu, 1958: 199).

The IRAA was, as Robert Butow (1961: 159) has written, 'an effort to mobilize totally the political, economic, ideological, cultural and spiritual resources of the nation so as to permit the government to do what it wished at home and abroad.' It thus ushered in an era during which government control extended into nearly every aspect of the people's lives, which would last until the end of World War II. The IRAA had branches in every village and town, calling on each person to join the war effort in some capacity, as members of such groups as the Imperial Rule Assistance Youth League, the Agriculturists' Patriotic Association, or the Writers' Patriotic Association (Duus, 1976: 222). The IRAA also oversaw the formation of the *tonarigumi*, or neighborhood associations, into which the entire nation was organized. These groups consisted of 10–20 households, which were required to hold monthly meetings, organize mutual defense teams, propagate government directives and oversee compulsory worship at local Shinto shrines. The *tonarigumi* also provided a basic unit for police control and mutual surveillance among neighbors.

As the government extended control into the neighborhoods, it also established more stringent guidelines for censorship and 'thought control,' blacklisting any book or article not in keeping with the nation's military goals. In 1933 and 1941, the Ministry of Education revised school textbooks to indoctrinate Japanese young people with nationalistic fervor. Imperial authority was elevated as the mythology of the founding of the nation by the Sun Goddess was presented as historical fact. By the late 1930s the nation was caught up in a mood of grim austerity, as anything Western was condemned. Even baseball, the national pastime, was curtailed, and a new Japanese term, *yakyu*, was coined to replace the borrowed word, '*besu-boru*.'

FRICTION WITH THE UNITED STATES

Amazingly, even as the atmosphere on the homefront turned increasingly anti-Western and anti-American, the Japanese leadership still looked to negotiations with the United States, China's most important source of international aid, as the likeliest way to end the 'China Problem' and to secure diplomatic access to Southeast Asian resources. Japan hoped for a negotiated withdrawal from China, which would nevertheless leave Japanese power firmly in place. What the Japanese believed would be a quick war in China had now dragged on for nearly four years, and meanwhile, the concern about the Soviet Union had not abated. The 'China Problem' was a serious drain on Japanese resources that was deflecting them from more important goals in the south.

Japan's Ambassador to the United States was Nomura Kichisaburo. An admiral, Nomura briefly served as Foreign Minister in the short-lived Abe Cabinet (30 August 1939–16 June 1940) and was selected as Ambassador in July 1940, partly because he and US President Franklin Delano Roosevelt had been acquaintances during World War I. Described by his negotiating partner, US Secretary of State Cordell Hull, as 'tall, robust, in fine health ... [and] ... honestly sincere' (quoted in Feis, 1950: 172), the two began discussions in Washington in March 1941.

Ambassador Nomura presented Japan's position: a negotiated troop withdrawal from China, the establishment of a joint Japanese–Chinese government in China by merging Chiang Kaishek's Nationalist government with that of the Japanese collaborator Wang Jingwei, Chinese recognition of Manchukuo, and a Japan–China anti-Soviet pact (Duus, 1976: 226). By mid-April, Secretary of State Hull responded with the US position: respect for the territorial integrity and sovereignty of all nations, non-interference in the internal affairs of other nations and preservation of the *status quo* in the Pacific unless change came about through peaceful means. The United States called for a return to the *status quo ante* 1931 which would require Japan to relinquish Manchukuo and unconditionally give up all claims in

China; in short, to turn their backs on the gains of the last ten years. The Japanese leadership of course found this totally unacceptable.

As Nomura negotiated in the United States, Matsuoka pursued his own agenda in Europe; he traveled to Italy and Germany to cement further the Tripartite Pact and, he hoped, to ameliorate Japan's relations with the Soviets by trading on their non-aggression treaty with Germany. The Germans were not willing to help Matsuoka secure improved relations with the Soviets. Matsuoka, apparently blind to the fact that German–Soviet relations were in a freefall, proceeded to Moscow where Stalin was only too happy to sign a neutrality pact with Japan on 13 April 1940, in which each nation pledged neutrality in the event that either was attacked by one or more powers.

As Nomura and Matsuoka pursued their separate and contradictory diplomatic agendas, Japanese military planners discussed the possibility of a military advance to the south.[4] The new pact with the Soviets alleviated the northern threat, freeing Japan to consider such a move.[5] But the real end to the Soviet threat came on 21 June 1941, when German armies invaded the Soviet Union, diverting Soviet attention away from its Siberian border with Manchukuo. Suddenly, a whole new vista opened for Japan and a liaison conference with the Emperor hastily convened to consider the new situation. Incredibly, Matsuoka, freshly returned from Moscow, advocated joining with Germany and attacking the Soviet Union. In whispers, Cabinet members increasingly questioned Matsuoka's sanity and met his suggestion with astonishment and consternation.

At an imperial conference at the beginning of July, the Cabinet settled on their response to the new situation. Japan would advance south regardless of any potential obstacles. 'In order to achieve her objectives [in the south],' the policy declared, 'Japan will not decline a war with England and the United States' (quoted in Butow, 1961: 219).

The Japanese leadership had now clearly faced the possibility of war with England and the United States. As former Foreign Minister Shigemitsu (1958: 237) wrote in his postwar memoir, 'This decision ... finally settled Japan's destiny. Unless the British and the Americans gave way, a clash was inevitable.' Japan's 'quick war' with China, begun without intention in 1937, had now, almost exactly four years later, metastasized into the fateful, and ultimately fatal, decision to consider war with England and the United States.

NOTES

[1]   Interestingly, Japan's right to conduct maneuvers here was not a new development. Rather, it dated back to the Boxer Protocol of 1901, in which China settled with foreign nations for the loss of life resulting from the anti-foreign Boxer Rebellion of 1900.

2   Konoe was the maternal grandfather of recent Japanese Prime Minister Hosokawa Morihiro, who took office in August 1993.
3   As Robert Butow (1961: 181–2) points out, an ironic twist led the three nations to conduct their negotiations in English, the language of their common enemies, because of the difficulty of the minute interpretations of Japanese, German and Italian.
4   Because American military intelligence had broken and was intercepting Japan's code, Secretary of State Hull was well aware of Japan's preparations even as he and Nomura negotiated.
5   In fact, Stalin is reputed to have given Matsuoka a bear-hug as he saw him off at the train station, telling him, 'Now Japan can move south' (Hane, 1992: 294).

CHAPTER SIX

JAPAN GOES TO WAR

By the summer of 1941, Japanese leaders were openly considering the possibility of war with the United States. The nation was firmly enmeshed in the Tripartite Alliance with Germany and Italy, and the Soviet threat had been eliminated by Hitler's Soviet invasion; Konoe's Cabinet discussed new opportunities. The decision was made to advance into Southeast Asia and secure access to the area's vast natural resources, recognizing that this courted war with the United States. Over the next several months, the Japanese leadership continued to discuss the implications of such a war. In December, Japanese bombers attacked Pearl Harbor, and the 'wanted, unwanted war' was begun. It was a war that would end four years later, when Japan faced the 'utter devastation' promised by the Potsdam Declaration.

THE FAILURE OF DIPLOMACY

During months of negotiations with the United States, Japan sought a satisfactory way to end its involvement in China, but there seemed to be no common grounds for understanding. While US Secretary of State Cordell Hull insisted that Japan return to the *status quo ante* 1931, Japanese resentments grew increasingly bitter. 'Success of this American policy,' read a February 1941 naval document on the possibility of war with the United States, 'would forever compel Japan, as in the past, to kowtow to the United States. With the sentinel of the Far East in economic chains, the Orient would once again become the playground of Western economic imperialists' (quoted in Crowley, 1970: 259). Newspapers, too, took up the anti-American message, promoting the 'Japan against the world' mentality. Japan's 'strategic requirements are absolute ... [the nation] must endure whatever difficulties it may meet in pursuit of our national policies,' read an editorial in the *Tokyo Asahi Shimbun* on 16 October 1941.

As it pondered these difficulties, the Konoe Cabinet underwent a reorganization. To get rid of Foreign Minister Matsuoka, increasingly viewed as a half-cocked pistol, the entire Cabinet resigned on 18 July 1941. Konoe immediately appointed a new Cabinet by reshuffling the old, *sans* Matsuoka.

The new Foreign Minister was Admiral Toyoda Teijiro, one of the three admirals and four generals who made up the 14-minister Cabinet. The reconstituted Cabinet upheld to the decisions made on 2 July: Konoe announced the formation of the new Cabinet to the nation, declaring, 'The policy of the country has already been fixed ... it now remains for us to put it into practice with decision and speed' (quoted in Tolischus, 1943: 167–8).

With decision and speed Konoe pursued the plan to occupy southern Indochina. While still involved in negotiations with the United States, Japan's Ambassador to Vichy France, Kato Sotomatsu, informed Pétain that Japan sought the use of eight Indochinese airfields, as well as the right to occupy both Saigon and Kamranh Bay. It was up to the Vichy government to decide whether this would be accomplished through diplomacy, in which case Japan pledged to respect French sovereignty in Indochina, or with force. As Matsuoka had indicated just before his forced resignation, Japan was determined to occupy southern Indochina 'despite any hindrances by Britain and America or even if the French or Indo-French authorities oppose it' (quoted in Feis, 1950: 224). Having thus secured an agreement with the Vichy government, Japan sent its forces south to Indochina on 21 July.

The United States had learned of such a possibility through the interception of a 'Magic' encryption in early July, and American reaction to Japan's southern advance was swift. On 26 July, President Roosevelt issued an executive order placing a total embargo on exports to Japan. In what was perhaps the biggest miscalculation of its entire war effort, Japan had wandered down the path to war with its most important trading partner. With 80 percent of its oil coming from the United States, the embargo, which of course included oil, now presented Japan with an 'ominous timetable.' According to calculations by the Japanese Supreme Command, without imported oil, the fleet could operate for no longer than two years. More importantly, after January 1941, Japan would be unable to launch an offensive operation. Using these calculations, the Supreme Command recommended that the decision for war be made before October 1941 (Crowley, 1970: 260). If Japan sat and did nothing, the Navy argued, its ability to wage war would slowly slip away. A quick strike in the South Pacific, while it might invite war with the United States and Britain, would gain Japan access to natural resources that would enable it to 'carry on a long war with all its hardship' (Shigemitsu, 1958: 249).

Still, the Japanese leadership negotiated with the United States. In August, Konoe proposed a one-on-one meeting with President Roosevelt. Roosevelt finally rejected the proposal in early September, having indicated that before such a meeting could occur, Japan would have to make concessions: withdrawal from the Tripartite Pact and troop withdrawal from North China and Inner Mongolia. In short, both sides remained firmly attached to their positions. At this juncture, historian Mikiso Hane (1992:

298) writes, 'It always seemed that just one additional step was necessary to consolidate the gains made with the previous step, until finally, after she had already stepped into southern Indochina, Japan was confronted with only two options: retreat or take the last fatal step forward.'

The Imperial Conference of 6 September 1941 formalized the determination not to retreat. The day before this conference the Emperor had an audience at which General Sugiyama Gen, Chief of the General Staff, and Admiral Nagano Osami, Chief of the Naval General Staff, presented their views on war with the United States. Sugiyama indicated that in the likely event that negotiations with the United States failed, Japan must be ready to go to war to secure Japan's oil supply. The South Pacific, he said, could be occupied in the space of three months. Uncharacteristically demonstrative, the Emperor replied angrily that the Army had said that the China problem would be settled in a month's time and yet the situation had dragged on now for over four years. How could the Army now promise to occupy an even larger and more remote area in three months? The Emperor demanded that such a weighty decision not be made without a tremendous effort toward a diplomatic solution. Moreover, the decision should be made not by the Supreme Command alone, but in concert with the Cabinet.

At the Imperial Conference, the Cabinet adopted the decision to go to war while at the same time continuing negotiations. If within a month no significant diplomatic progress was made, war preparations would commence. Once again, in an uncharacteristic interjection, the Emperor responded to the decision by reading a poem written by his grandfather, the Emperor Meiji, calling to attention his grandfather's love of peace:

> All the seas, in every quarter,
>   are as brothers to one another.
> Why then, do the winds and waves of strife
>   rage so turbulently throughout the world? (quoted in Butow, 1961: 258)

But the decision was made and the meeting adjourned. The two apparently contradictory approaches, preparing for war on the one hand and pursuing negotiations on the other, would march forward. Both the Emperor and Konoe, following the constitutional dictum of the Independence of the Supreme Command, viewed the government and the military as two separate entities: while one pursued peace, the other prepared for war. Konoe's government had surrendered to the military.

The very evening of the Imperial Conference, Konoe met for dinner with the US Ambassador to Japan, Joseph Grew. Aware that such a meeting might provoke the fatal wrath of the military, Konoe arranged that the dinner be held in utmost secrecy. With unrealistic optimism Konoe continued to hold out hope that negotiations with the United States could be successful. But the time was short – he had a mere month to achieve what had eluded Japan for the last four years. Ambassador Grew's own grasp of the situation was more realistic, as demonstrated in a cable he sent just weeks earlier: 'the possibility that the constructive statesmen of Japan will be able to counteract the increasing psychology of desperation is at present diminishing daily. Traditionally in this country a *national psychology of desperation develops into a determination to risk all*' (quoted in Butow, 1961: 245n). Konoe's dinner with Grew was unproductive.

When in early October the Japanese government received another note from Secretary of State Hull outlining US demands for withdrawal from China, it was clear that negotiations had failed. Again the Cabinet met to consider the decision of the Imperial Conference a month earlier. Now, the Navy, which would have to be at the forefront of any attack on the United States, stalled, fearing it was not at present equal to the task. Navy leaders, however, were reluctant to make this pronouncement officially, not wanting to be singled out for a failure of nerve against the US. In a wild turn-about of the Independence of the Supreme Command, so important hitherto, Minister of the Navy Oikawa Koshiro and a number of his fellow officers turned to Konoe to make the final call, which Konoe was loath to do. In any event, Minister of War General Tojo Hideki insisted that the momentous decision was not the Prime Minister's to make. In the face of this deadlock, Konoe and his entire Cabinet resigned.

In this crisis, Tojo emerged as the candidate who best understood the situation and had the best chance of maintaining control over the army. Tojo (1884–1948) was a native of Tokyo and a graduate of the Military Academy. In 1937 he had served as Chief of Staff of the Kwantung Army and thus was thoroughly acquainted with Japan's situation in China. A leading figure in the Tosei, or Control Faction, which had long advocated war with China, Tojo had served as Konoe's War Minister since 1940. Extremely intelligent – his nickname was 'Razor Brain' – Tojo was decisive and quick-tempered (Feis, 1950: 81). He assumed the premiership on 17 October, while retaining his position as War Minister. Now civil and military matters were united in one man.

With Tojo newly in office, an Imperial Conference on 5 November now determined a timeline for war with the United States: if by 1 December negotiations had produced no satisfactory outcome, Japan would go to war shortly thereafter. The conferees outlined two proposals to submit to the US. When the first was rejected, as was expected, the second and last proposal, which called on the US to ensure Japan access to oil in exchange for a Japanese withdrawal from French Indochina, was put forth on 20 November. Two days later, before an American response, the Navy began to assemble the force that would attack Pearl Harbor.

The American response to Japan's second proposal came on 26 November when Secretary of State Hull delivered to Nomura his 'comprehensive basic proposal.' In it, he reiterated the US position calling for a return to the *status quo ante* 1931.[1] In light of Japan's mood and the decisions already made at the Imperial Conference three weeks earlier, the Japanese viewed this 'Hull Note' as an ultimatum. In any event, the naval task force based at Etorofu, on the Kurile Islands, had already been instructed to set sail toward Hawaii.[2]

From Washington, Nomura continued to urge his government to keep trying to negotiate; if negotiations were to be ended, he added, 'it would be best not to keep up a false front of friendliness, and to strike from behind it.' Tojo responded saying that in light of the Hull Note, 'talks will be de facto ruptured. This is inevitable. However, I do not wish you to give the impression that the negotiations are broken off ... From now on do the best you can' (quoted in Feis, 1950: 327–8). Meanwhile, in Tokyo, Tojo called an extraordinary meeting with the Cabinet and senior statesmen, including eight former prime ministers. Though several of the former prime ministers, including Konoe, expressed serious concern over the decision to go to war, none were willing to oppose openly the decision for war. Two days later, in a conference with the Emperor, the Cabinet, together with the Supreme Command, made the decision to go to war. The next day, the Army and Navy Chiefs of Staff reported to the Emperor the date for the attack: 8 December (Japanese time).

WAR

'Air Raid On Pearl Harbor. This Is No Drill,' read the 7 December radio broadcast to Washington and all US forces on sea (quoted in Toland, 1970: 216). At 7:50 a.m., Sunday 7 December, the carrier-based Japanese attack on Pearl Harbor commenced. Though the Japanese Foreign Ministry had insisted on a proper declaration of war, bungling at the Japanese Embassy in Washington meant the United States received no prior notification. Un-aware of the precise time the attack would begin, Nomura waited for the secretary to type the 14-part document he would present to Hull, post-poning his slated 1:00 p.m. meeting with Hull for one hour. (Okumura Katsuzo, who struggled over the typing for five hours that morning, was a diplomatic secretary, not a stenographic secretary, as security concerns required that the document be typed by an individual with top clearance.) Arriving at Hull's office at 2:00 p.m., Nomura was ushered in 20 minutes later, still ignorant of the fact that just one hour earlier, his government had launched its attack. (In 1941, Washington time was five and a *half* hours later than Hawaii time.) Hull, however, had learned of the attack just 15 minutes earlier, and after listening to Nomura's business, the enraged but calm Secretary sent Nomura back to his Embassy, where the Japanese ambassador learned at last that the war had begun.

Though it had been clear to US intelligence that Japan was planning some sort of military attack in the immediate future, none believed the attack would, or indeed *could* be against Pearl Harbor. The US Navy simply did not believe that Japan was capable of launching a carrier-based attack so far from its home islands. The President, too, though alive to the possibility of attack on an American installation somewhere, also misjudged the location. Just half an hour before the bombing, Roosevelt, in a meeting with Chinese ambassador Hu Shih, indicated his expectation that Japan might attack Malaya, Thailand, the Dutch East Indies or maybe even the Philippines sometime during the next 48 hours.

In the space of the two-hour attack, Japanese bombers destroyed or damaged 18 American ships, most of the American Pacific fleet. The attack also wiped out 188 planes, damaging an additional 159. Almost 2,500 Americans died, and nearly 1,200 were wounded. Japanese losses, on the other hand, were much smaller: 29 planes, 5 midget submarines, and 100 casualties (Hane, 1992: 310). It seemed a stunning victory. But from a long-range point of view, Japan's methods at Pearl Harbor redounded to their ultimate failure. Targeting ships rather than permanent installations, like oil tanks, enabled the United States to recover relatively quickly after the initial shock was over. Most importantly, the choice of Pearl Harbor galvanized American public opinion, producing a hard-edged determination to fight the Japanese, and an immediate declaration of war against Japan.

Japan's choice of Pearl Harbor, however, fitted into its overall military strategy. Japanese naval strategists realized their most important aim was to gain immediately an upper hand that would enable Japan to secure the resources vital to a longer fight. After the initial hard strike, Japan would proceed to establish a defense ring around its home islands. Since war with the US seemed inevitable, Japanese planners believed a quick preemptive strike was necessary to destroy as much US fighting potential as possible. The fact that the US had so far refrained from directly entering the war in Europe, despite its strong ties there, indicated a firm commitment to isolationism. The hope was that the US, already a reluctant fighter, would be weakened and brought to the negotiating table, now ready to compromise, and Japan could avoid the prospect of a lengthy war. Admiral Nagano, Chief of the Navy General Staff, had himself admitted that the chance of victory was uncertain if the war lasted three years (Toland, 1970: 125).

The first six months of the war brought a chronicle of Japanese success. Concurrent with the attack on Pearl Harbor, Japanese forces undertook military operations against US, British and Dutch positions in the Philippines, Malaya, and elsewhere in the South Pacific. Just days after the attack on Pearl Harbor, Japanese submarines and bombers destroyed the new British battleship, the *Prince of Wales*, the largest in the world, and a heavy cruiser, the *Repulse*, at Singapore, virtually wiping out Britain's Far Eastern defenses. Before the end of December, Japanese forces controlled the American possessions of Guam and Wake Island as well as Britain's Hong Kong. Another two months' time saw the British surrender of Singapore and the Malay Peninsula. By early March, the Dutch were forced to capitulate their position in the East Indies. Since they had been unable to destroy the oil fields there before being ousted, Japan had now won access to the oil supplies it so desperately needed. After fierce fighting around the Philippine Islands, this American stronghold fell to Japanese control in early May. By mid-May, Japan wrested control of Burma, cutting off Allied supplies to China. Thus in just six months of fighting, Japan had carved out an astounding ring of victories spanning from Burma to Wake Island.

This succession of quick victories surprised even the Japanese, and presented military planners with exciting but difficult questions. The Army and Navy Chiefs of Staff found they were at odds with one another on how best to take advantage of Japan's early victories. At a liaison conference in March 1942, the Army argued in favor of consolidating its current gains in anticipation of the US counterattack, expected to come sometime in 1943. The Navy, on the other hand, though it had initially dragged its feet over starting the war, was now so exhilarated with its accomplishments that it advocated expanding into Australia. After two weeks of intense discussion, a compromise was eventually worked out. Members of the Army General Staff convinced the Navy to abandon its visions of invading Australia, while agreeing to a naval plan to conquer islands off the Australian coast – Fiji, Samoa and New Caledonia.

Admiral Yamamoto Isoroku (1884–1943), chief architect of Japan's attack on Pearl Harbor, however, refused to be reigned in by this compromise and pursued plans for another direct attack on American territory, this time at Midway Island. Earlier in his career Yamamoto had served as naval attaché in Washington; a sailor under his command during the war reported that Yamamoto, having seen the 'automobile plants in Detroit and the oilfields of Texas,' believed it would be 'foolish to fight a war against America' (quoted in Cook and Cook, 1992: 82). Even before the war began Yamamoto had argued that Japan could not fight a sustained war against the United States, and advocated a lightening quick strategy. Now, he swore, if he was not allowed to carry out his plan he would resign.

In-fighting and disagreement between Army and Navy planners was a serious problem that plagued Japan's military planning throughout the war. Indeed, it was this problem to which Army General (and Prime Minister) Tojo himself assigned the reason for Japan's defeat. As a prisoner in Sugamo Prison after the war, Tojo wrote:

> Basically it [the reason for defeat] was lack of co-ordination ... the Supreme Command was divided between the Army and the Navy – two entities that would not work in unison. I did not hear of the Midway

defeat till more than a month after it occurred. Even now I do not know
the details. There was no proper unity in operations right up to the finish.
(quoted in Shigemitsu, 1958: 271)

Having secured a grudging agreement from the Army General Staff,
and bolstered by the early May sinking of the American carrier the
Lexington and damage to the carrier the *Yorktown* at the Battle of the
Coral Sea, Yamamoto planned for the attack on the Midway Islands. His
objective was to finish what he had begun at Pearl Harbor: to destroy the
remaining US Pacific fleet. But American intelligence succeeded in breaking
the Japanese code, working feverishly throughout the month of May to
ascertain Japanese plans. On 20 May 1942 the Combat Intelligence Unit
under Rear-Admiral Chester Nimitz intercepted a lengthy directive from
Yamamoto that revealed Japanese plans for a major offensive in the Pacific.
Unsure whether the target would be Oahu or Midway, Intelligence con-
cocted a report detailing the breakdown of a water plant on Midway. Two
days later, Japanese transmissions reported a malfunctioning water plant at
their target, confirming for the United States that Midway was indeed the
focus of Japanese plans.

Armed with this knowledge, Nimitz had a month secretly to fortify
American defenses at Midway, aware that his force of two carriers (a third,
the *Yorktown*, was slated for three months of repair work), eight cruisers
and 17 destroyers would be inferior to Japan's force. In early June, as a
diversionary tactic, Japan launched an attack on the Aleutian Islands while
Admiral Nagumo led four aircraft carriers to Midway. Yamamoto followed
Nagumo, intending to attack the American ships as they rushed south from
their engagement in the Aleutians. When the fighting at Midway began on
the morning of 4 June, Japanese plans were to focus on bombing the islands
themselves. But when suddenly faced with three American carriers – the
Yorktown had been brought back into service by round-the-clock repair
efforts – the Japanese hastily attempted to change plans and focus on the
US carriers while themselves under constant air attack. In the end, Japan's
four carriers were destroyed, along with one heavy cruiser and 332 planes.
Over 3,500 Japanese died in the battle, including 100 Navy pilots. Under
the conditions of Japan's wartime economy, Japan was unable to recover
from the devastating loss of its four carriers, which were never replaced.
The pilots, too, were irreplaceable and throughout the war Japan faced a
chronic shortage of experienced pilots. The Battle of Midway was the
Japanese Navy's last offensive action; the tide of war began to turn against
Japan.

JAPAN ON THE DEFENSIVE

By late summer 1942, fighting focused on Japan's most forward position at Guadalcanal on the Solomon Islands, east of New Guinea. For six months, Japanese forces fought a war of attrition with US Marines. Although the United States lost four aircraft carriers in the fighting, Japanese supply lines failed; by February 1943, Japan was driven from Guadalcanal, or, as the characteristically euphemistic official Japanese announcement put it, Japan was forced to 'amend the line of advance' (Shigemitsu, 1958: 278). The United States now adopted an 'island-hopping' campaign designed to re-claim control over the Pacific. Nimitz would lead the Navy and Marine Corps in the central Pacific while General Douglas MacArthur would lead the Army from New Guinea to the Philippines.

Japan's situation was also damaged by German defeats in Europe. In February 1943, Hitler's army was forced out of Stalingrad after a horribly costly year-long siege. Just months later, Mussolini's power in Italy crum-bled, and Italy surrendered to the Allies in September 1943. Despite the Tripartite Pact, the three nations had never coordinated their military strategies – indeed, some historians argue that had they done so, the out-come of the war might have been very different. Nevertheless, Japanese strategy did rely on German success at undercutting the strength of the Allied forces. In April 1943, Japan received another devastating blow when the plane that was carrying Yamamoto to the Solomon Islands for a morale-boosting campaign was shot down.

The success of Nimitz's island-hopping campaign brought the Gilbert Islands under Allied control in November 1943; four months later the Allies gained control over the Marshall Islands. The battle for the Marshall Islands was horribly costly for the Japanese side; each American death brought an estimated 17 Japanese deaths. In a similar vein, the March 1944 Japanese Army offensive against India, designed to stop the flow of British and American supplies to Nationalist China over the 'Hump' (the air route over the Himalayas), was tragically characteristic of Japan's blind determin-ation to fight regardless of cost. With no plan for resupplying his troops, General Mutaguchi, commander of the 15th Army, went ahead and launched the campaign. Heading into battle with inadequate weapons and insufficient ammunition, Mutaguchi instructed his troops to forage for food along the way. But faced with British air superiority, the campaign was doomed from the start. Fighting continued for four months, until the men, with their nearly mutinous sub-commanders, retreated to Burma. Of the 100,000 men who started the campaign, 30,000 died in combat, and another 20,000 died of disease and starvation. 'This ridiculous offensive,' Japanese historian Ienaga Saburo (1978: 147) would later write, 'was a miniature version of the Pacific War.'

In the summer of 1944, the Mariana Islands, once the center of Japan's naval defense, became the target of Allied attack. The ghastly fighting for this key position left over 50,000 Japanese dead, including 10,000 civilians who, like their military counterparts, committed suicide rather than submit to the invading forces. Establishing control over the Mariana Islands, which Prime Minister Tojo had once called an 'impregnable fortress' (quoted in Cook and Cook, 1992: 281), now enabled the US to build a naval base on Guam, and more devastatingly, air bases at Tinian and Saipan. From these bases the US was able to launch air raids on the Japanese home islands.

The first such attack occurred in November 1944, when 80 B-29 bombers roared above Tokyo. By early spring 1945, after the fall of Iwo Jima, situated halfway between Saipan and Tokyo, the US stepped up aerial attacks on Japan, with fire-bombing campaigns against major cities. On a single night in early March, incendiary bombs dropped on Tokyo killed 78,000 people, injured over 43,000 and left 1.5 million homeless (Duus, 1976: 232). Similar attacks left Osaka, Yokohama, Kobe and Nagoya in tatters. For the Japanese people, the war had come home as never before.

THE HOME FRONT

When the news of Pearl Harbor broke, a few Japanese, like Kwantung Army fighter pilot Mogami Sadao, harbored misgivings. Reacting to the news, Mogami asked himself, 'What! War with America! Can we win against America?' But the vast majority heard the news with euphoria and elation: the months of tense waiting were finally over. Itabashi Koshu, a high school student at the time, remembered, 'I felt as if my blood boiled and my flesh quivered. The whole nation bubbled over, excited and inspired' (both quoted in Cook and Cook, 1992: 77, 85).

In the euphoria, the Japanese people threw themselves into the war effort. The *tonarigumi*, neighborhood organizations of 10–20 households that encompassed every neighborhood in Japan, worked to ensure proper commitment to the war. The *tonarigumi*, for example, staged send-off parties at which mothers, wives and daughters, festooned with white sashes bearing the message 'Congratulations on Being Called to Service,' cheered as they sent their men off to war. With the men gone to battle, those who remained behind did what they could to support the war effort. Children as young as 12 and 13 were recruited to work in the factories. High school girls, told they would be 'defeating America with these arms,' worked long hours, fashioning lacquered paper balloons to launch into the jet stream to carry bombs across the Pacific (Cook and Cook, 1992: 190). By 1943, Sunday became a workday like any other.

Those men not actively involved in the war were nevertheless called upon to adopt a quasi-military uniform: a khaki suit with wrapped leggings, topped with a peaked khaki cap. Women wore *monpe*, baggy bloomers. The dreariness created by this drab dress was reflected in the landscape of wartime urban Japan. Well before the war was close to Japan's home islands, Tokyo citizens were instructed to maintain a nightly blackout and to dig bomb shelters. As the government poured its resources into the military, civilian life suffered. Robert Guillain (1981: 118), a French journalist who lived in Japan from 1938 to 1946, wrote of Tokyo in 1943:

> The subway was a wreck; rusty trolley cars seemed to jounce on square wheels; train windows were broken, baggage racks sagged, seats were eviscerated; public phones were worn out; bicycles wobbled on flat tires; rattletrap autos were abandoned in the streets.

Despite all the resources being poured into the war, industrial production was abysmal. On the economic front, Japan's war effort seemed doomed from the start. Historian Mikiso Hane (1992: 331) wrote that 'The major single element in Japan's military defeat was the collapse of her economy.' Access to raw materials, a problem Japan had sought to ameliorate with its war, was never easy: it has been estimated that the United States possessed 78 times more of the natural resources necessary to prosecuting the war than Japan. The glaring disparity is especially obvious in the key industry of aircraft production. Between 1941 and 1944, the United States produced nearly 262,000 airplanes while Japan produced about 59,000. Moreover, as the quality of American aircraft improved, Japanese quality declined (Cook and Cook, 1992: 171).

Journalists penned a steady stream of heroic stories from the battlefields, but also told of the ordinary boys, the sons of ordinary mothers, heading off to the front to do their duty for the Emperor. Much of what the journalists wrote, however, was simply not true. As one journalist explained years after the war,

> In hindsight, a lot of the announcements from the Imperial General Headquarters look like nothing but lies. [Official information all had to have the Imperial seal on it.] Back then it was inconceivable that the Emperor could make a mistake. He was a god. You couldn't change what he'd said and explain that it was in error. Once something had been announced, they'd have to try to justify it, and one lie would lead to another, until the whole thing became a big lie. (quoted in Cook and Cook, 1992: 217)

This aura of untruth, of tight-lipped control over information, manifested itself in renewed repression of the population. The Peace Preservation Law, the 1925 legislation designed to give the government a measure of control over the newly expanded electorate, now became a ready tool for wielding a tighter rein on the population. Previously used to proscribe radical political activity, in 1941 the law was expanded to target unaffiliated liberal intellectuals, and those who refused to espouse the official state Shinto. Most chillingly, the revised law allowed for 'preventative arrest.' From 1928 to the end of 1943, enforcement of the Peace Preservation Law accounted for the arrest of some 68,500 people (not including arrests in Japan's colonies in Korea and Taiwan). About one-tenth of these would eventually be tried and convicted, each spending a minimum of six months in prison. One reporter for the *Mainichi* newspaper, Japan's largest, was arrested for writing an editorial in which he called upon the nation to produce more airplanes, questioning whether Japan could really win the war using bamboo spears (Cook and Cook, 1992: 221–2). The Special Higher Police, or thought police, were in charge of such arrests. As wartime Foreign Minister Shigemitsu (1958: 299) recalled,

> It was a 'total war': kill or be killed. The Army was resolved to fight to the very end. If anyone spoke of making peace before that, he was ruthlessly punished. The War Minister [Tojo] rigidly enforced the autocratic powers of the Army and used the gendarmerie as state police. To them a peace advocate was a pacifist and anyone who mentioned defeat was a rebel and such people were to be suppressed.

THE END IN SIGHT

The fall of Saipan in July 1944 brought serious consequences for Japan, both politically and militarily. For Tojo, it meant the end of his career as Prime Minister. As the war situation worsened, Tojo had responded by taking greater control over the Cabinet. In 1943 he established and headed a munitions ministry in an effort to ameliorate the conflict between the always rivalrous Army and Navy, then competing with one another for dwindling war resources. The lack of coordination between these two branches was stunning: 'they refused to standardize equipment, with the result that an otherwise identical item might require left-hand threaded screws if supplied to the Navy and right-hand threaded screws if supplied to the Army' (Duus, 1976: 233–4). In February 1944, Tojo made a last-ditch effort to deal with the problem by naming himself the military Chief of Staff. But within months the retreat from Burma and the fall of Saipan brought the growing dissatisfaction with his Cabinet to a head. Responding to a resolution passed by a group of seven former premiers that called for the resignation of his entire Cabinet, Tojo stepped down in mid-July 1944. He was replaced by General Koiso Kuniaki, who returned to Japan from his post as Governor-General of Korea to assume the position. Koiso, who believed from the start of his tenure that Japan had already lost the war, served as Prime Minister until the final months of the war.

Militarily as well, the fall of Saipan was a devastating blow for Japan. As the Allies made plans for an assault on the Philippines, Japan prepared a desperate weapon: kamikaze pilots. Vice-Admiral Onishi Takijiro, arriving at Luzon (the northern-most of the Philippine Islands) in the fall of 1944, found fewer than 100 functioning planes available for the defense of the Philippine Islands. Faced with this dire situation, he determined there was 'only one way of channeling our meager strength into maximum efficiency, and that is to organize suicide attack units composed of Zero fighters equipped with 250-kilogram bombs, with each plane to crash-dive into an enemy carrier' (quoted in Toland, 1970: 568). Although isolated kamikaze attacks had been launched at American ships earlier, none had met their target. Now, in October 1944, as Allied forces converged at Leyte Gulf poised to attack the Philippines, the Japanese rallied this weapon of last resort.

The naval bombardment of Leyte began at dawn on the morning of 20 October, and within hours 60,000 Allied ground troops had landed. Over the course of the four-day battle, Japan lost 'three battleships, four carriers, six heavy cruisers, three light cruisers, eight destroyers, and six submarines' (Hane, 1992: 328). Despite the desperate kamikaze tactics, Japan's Navy was virtually destroyed and its home islands now lay open to the possibility of Allied air attack. One month later, the fire-bombing campaigns against Japanese cities began.

By January 1945, Allied forces made a landing on Luzon, taking the island by 4 March. As this fighting raged, Nimitz led naval forces to Iwo Jima, an eight square-mile island of tremendous strategic importance situated halfway between Saipan and Tokyo. United States Marines landed on the rocky beaches of Iwo Jima in mid-February and found themselves immediately engaged in a pitched battle that finally culminated in one-on-one combat. The battle cost the United States nearly 7,000 dead and virtually wiped out the Japanese garrison of 22,500 soldiers.

By April, the two-pronged Allied attack was ready to converge on the island of Okinawa, the 'strategic gateway to the Japanese heartland' (Butow, 1954: 58). The German surrender on 7 May meant that Japan now became the Allies' sole military focus. As the Japanese Army bore the brutal onslaught, the Supreme Council for the Direction of the War, comprising the Prime Minister, the Foreign Minister, the Ministers of War and of the Navy, and the Chiefs of the Army and Navy General Staff,[3] met with other military leaders in Tokyo on 6 June to discuss the situation facing the nation. These men discussed and adopted 'The Fundamental Policy to be Followed Henceforth in the Conduct of the War,' which, in effect, committed the nation to fighting to the last man (Butow, 1954: 93). Two days later, in an Imperial Conference, the Emperor effectively ratified the decision. As Allied forces tightened the noose on Okinawa, thousands of civilians committed group suicide to avoid capture. When the battle ended on 22 June, some 110,000 Japanese soldiers and 100,000 civilians lay dead.

Commanding General Ushijima Mitsuru died by his own hand, committing hara-kiri at the end of the battle (Hane, 1992: 330). 'The scene was now set for the battle for the homeland. The Army ... planned to lead the nation into battle and busied itself laying in stocks of bamboo spears and wooden guns' (Shigemitsu, 1958: 354).

While Okinawans faced actual combat conditions, Japanese elsewhere were not spared the devastating effects of enemy warfare. Throughout the spring of 1945, fire-bombing campaigns rained destruction on Japanese cities. During a single night in early March, as many as 100,000 Tokyo civilians died in the air raids, 'probably the single greatest loss of life in a single day from military action in that or any other war, including the atomic bombings' (Cook and Cook, 1992: 350). Throughout the country, food was short and malnutrition rampant – the Japanese, including military personnel, were getting an average of 1,050 calories per day on rationed food. Younger urban children were evacuated to the countryside, where they were safe from the air raids, but no better fed. Boys as young as 15 were recruited for military service, while women, children and the elderly trained with bamboo spears to fight off the anticipated invasion of the home islands. A 'conviction that there was no escape from a fight to the death gradually took hold of the people. They were too exhausted to think clearly' (Shigemitsu, 1958: 335).

Just days after the invasion of Okinawa began, Prime Minister Koiso resigned. The highly respected senior statesman Suzuki Kantaro took his place. As a retired admiral, Suzuki's nomination represented a continuation of the movement away from having the premier be a general on active service that had begun with the appointment of Koiso; this seemed a challenge to the fanatically war-minded Army. Suzuki appointed as his Foreign Minister Togo Shigenori. Togo had occupied that post at the time of Pearl Harbor, and had, in Suzuki's words, 'been opposed to the war from the very beginning and ... resigned from the Tojo Cabinet as a measure of opposition to Tojo's dictatorial and high-handed policies' (quoted in Butow, 1954: 65). As a result, wrote former Foreign Minister Shigemitsu (1958: 353) in his memoirs, 'Thinking people hoped that this would be a Peace Cabinet.' Nevertheless, even among senior statesmen, any discussion of peace could be considered treasonous. Shortly after Suzuki's appointment, War Minister Anami arrested 400 people suspected of being peace advocates; included in this number was former Ambassador to England (and future Prime Minister) Yoshida Shigeru. Meanwhile, the Army continued to promote vociferously the inevitability of a final (and clearly suicidal) battle on the Japanese home islands.

Those in the Cabinet who very quietly advocated peace held out hope for Soviet mediation in ending the war. But unbeknownst to them, the Soviet Union was bound by terms discussed at Yalta in February to enter the war against Japan within three months of the German surrender in exchange for territorial concessions in China and the northern Pacific. Japanese overtures to the Soviets in April were rebuffed when the Soviet Union announced that it would not extend the two nations' Neutrality Pact. The surreptitious nature of the peace advocates' activities made their efforts virtually impotent in the face of the harangue of the militarists. Hanging on to such slim evidence as 'shadows of deep concern' on the Emperor's face as evidence of his favoring a quick peace, Lord Keeper of the Privy Seal Kido Koin understood that the only player powerful enough to oppose the militarists was the Emperor himself. In effect, Kido was formulating a plan whereby the Emperor would lead a civil end-run around the military, thus re-establishing civilian power in the government. In mid-June Kido approached the Emperor to sound him out on the issue of Japan's ending the war 'with honor,' and after their private conversation he felt 'deeply satisfied' that the Emperor supported a quick end to the war (Butow, 1954: 114). But when the Emperor called for an Imperial Conference on 22 June 1945 – the day Okinawa fell – his words to the assembled group were too vague, asking whether it were not time to 'consider other methods of coping with the crisis facing the nation' (quoted in Butow, 1954: 119). The end result of this meeting was yet another fruitless overture to the Soviets at the end of June.

Meanwhile, the Allies were preparing for their meeting at Potsdam, to convene on 17 July, at which Harry S. Truman, Clement Atlee, Josef Stalin and Chiang Kaishek would discuss the end of the war against Japan. On 26 July, the Allies issued the Potsdam Declaration reiterating their demand for Japan's unconditional surrender and promising that 'the prodigious land, sea and air forces of the United States, the British Empire, and of China ... are poised to strike the final blows upon Japan.' Resistance would only mean 'the inevitable and complete destruction of the Japanese armed forces and just as inevitably the utter devastation of the Japanese homeland' (quoted in Butow, 1954: 243).

When the Cabinet and the Supreme Council for the Direction of the War met the day after the Potsdam Declaration was issued, the most Prime Minister Suzuki and Foreign Minister Togo could do in the face of the military's demand for an absolute rejection of the Declaration was to advocate taking a 'wait and see' approach and for the time being to ignore the Allies' demand. At a press conference about the Potsdam Declaration the next day, Prime Minister Suzuki stated that 'The government does not regard it as a thing of great value; the government will ignore it. We will press forward resolutely to carry the war to a successful conclusion' (quoted in Butow, 1954: 148).

Naturally, the Allies interpreted this as an outright rejection of the Declaration, and began to plan accordingly to 'strike the final blows' on a

1. Suffragettes in Japan in 1929 expounding their demand for voting power during municipal elections in Tokyo.
Photo: Peter Newark's Historical Pictures.

2. Japanese invasion of Manchuria, 1933.
Photo: Peter Newark's Historical Pictures.

3. Emperor of Japan inspecting the huge trumpet-like aircraft detectors, part of Japan's air defences circa 1935. Photo: Peter Newark's Historical Pictures.

4. Japanese women in traditional dress, 1937.
Photo: Peter Newark's Historical Pictures.

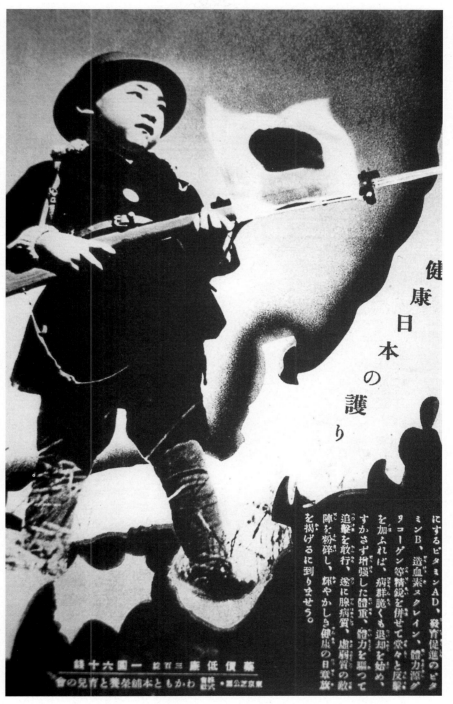

5. Young Japan undergoing military training: Japanese poster of 1938.
Photo: Peter Newark's Historical Pictures.

6. WWII Japanese aircraft production circa 1941.
Photo: Peter Newark's Historical Pictures.

7. WWII Japanese troops victorious on Bataan in the spring of 1942.
Photo: Peter Newark's Historical Pictures.

8. Japanese POW being questioned after capture on Okinawa in April 1945.
Photo: Peter Newark's Historical Pictures.

9. Japanese officials on board USS Missouri in Tokyo Bay, 2nd September 1945: MacArthur reads terms of surrender. Photo: Peter Newark's Historical Pictures.

10. Tokyo, 1945.
Photo: Peter Newark's Historical Pictures.

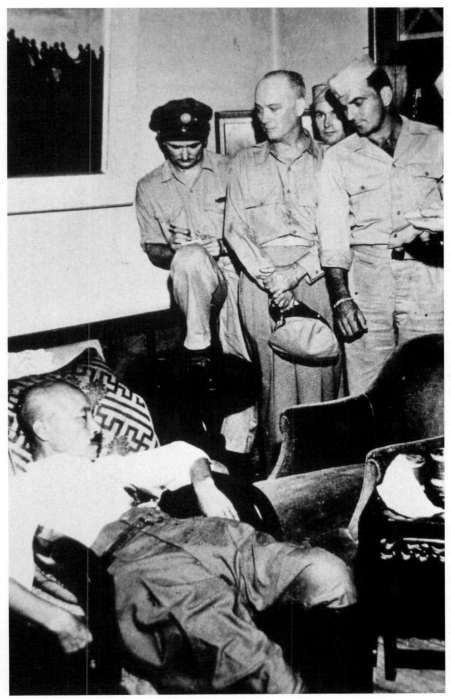

11. Hideki Tojo slumped in an armchair after attempting to shoot himself,
11th September 1945.
Photo: Peter Newark's Historical Pictures.

12. Hiroshima six months after the atom bomb: rough shacks have been built on the ruins. Photo: Peter Newark's Historical Pictures.

recalcitrant Japan. US President Truman, who assumed office in April after the death of Franklin Roosevelt, was faced with choosing between two alternatives: a land invasion of the Japanese islands, or use of the atomic bomb. At that point, Japanese troops were pouring into southern Kyushu; by August, 900,000 Japanese troops were in place, with more being transported to the area in anticipation of a 1 November invasion date. At the time the United States would have been able to muster 765,000 troops, nowhere near the desired ratio (Ferrell, 1998: 110). Believing the Japanese would resist an invasion down to the last man, woman and child, Truman turned to the atomic bomb. Originally designed for use against Germany, the German surrender in May had obviated that option. The first successful test of an atomic bomb took place in July, and the United States had only two in its arsenal.

On 6 August, at 8:15 in the morning, the American aircraft *Enola Gay* released its atomic cargo over the city of Hiroshima. The destruction was instantaneous and devastating. In Tokyo that evening, the newspapers, which had treated even the worst of the fire-bombing with cavalier lightness, published headlines that escaped censorship: 'New Type of Bomb Strikes Hiroshima: Much Damage.' Over 87,000 died in the blast, and 50,000 more died of radiation sickness over the course of the next few months (Cook and Cook, 1992: 383).

On 9 August, Stalin upheld his pledge made at Yalta and Soviet troops streamed into Manchuria. In the face of this development, the Supreme Council on the Direction of the War met to discuss Japanese options. In the midst of their meeting, they received news of the atomic attack on Nagasaki.[4] Still, Army leaders would not budge and the meeting ended with no resolution. A Cabinet meeting later that same day also ended in deadlock. Finally, at an Imperial Conference convened near midnight, in the Emperor's underground air raid shelter, the President of the Privy Council, Hiranuma, in unknowing alliance with Prime Minister Suzuki, prevailed upon the Emperor to make a final decision on the matter. The Emperor agreed with advocates of peace, saying:

> I have given serious thought to the situation prevailing at home and abroad and have concluded that continuing the war can only mean destruction for the nation and a prolongation of bloodshed and cruelty in the world. I cannot bear to see my innocent people suffer any longer. Ending the war is the only way to restore world peace and to relieve the nation from the terrible distress with which it is burdened ... I swallow my own tears and give my sanction to the proposal to accept the Allied proclamation ... (reconstructed[5] in Butow, 1954: 175–6)

The assembled group made the decision to accept the Potsdam Declaration with the proviso that it not in any way compromise the prerogatives of the Emperor.

Japan's first surrender offer, containing this exception, was delivered to the United States on 10 August. The Allied reply, coming from US Secretary of State James F. Byrnes, stated that 'the authority of the Emperor and the Japanese Government to rule the state shall be subject to the Supreme Commander of the Allied powers' (quoted in Butow, 1954: 245). This, Byrnes felt, would enable the Japanese to retain the Emperor, if that was in accordance with the 'freely expressed will of the Japanese people,' as stated in the Potsdam Declaration, while still allowing the Allies to set the terms.

Once again, the Japanese leadership was faced with a decision. Because Byrnes's reply did not explicitly guarantee protection for the Emperor or the imperial institution, the militarists were adamantly opposed. In a repeat of the earlier process, the Supreme Council for the Direction of the War met again on 13 August. Again, at this meeting, the War Minister and the chiefs of the Army and the Navy refused to agree to the Allied demand and the group deadlocked. Again the Cabinet met and again the Cabinet deadlocked. Once again, an Imperial Conference convened. At 10:50 on the morning of 14 August, the Emperor met with his Cabinet, the Supreme Council for the Direction of the War, and other high state officials. The Emperor spoke last:

> I appreciate how difficult it will be for the officers and men of the Army and Navy to surrender their arms to the enemy and to see their homeland occupied. Indeed, it is difficult for me to issue the order making this necessary and to deliver so many of my trusted servants into the hands of the Allied authorities by whom they will be accused of being war criminals. In spite of these feelings, so difficult to bear, I cannot endure the thought of letting my people suffer any longer. A continuation of the war would bring death to tens, perhaps even hundreds of thousands of persons. The whole nation would be reduced to ashes. How then could I carry on the wishes of my imperial ancestors?
>
> The decision I have reached is akin to the one forced upon my Grandfather, the Emperor Meiji, at the time of the Triple Intervention. As he endured the unendurable, so shall I, and so must you.
>
> It is my desire that you, my Ministers of State, accede to my wishes and forthwith accept the Allied reply [surrender conditions]. In order that the people may know of my decision, I request you to prepare at once an imperial rescript so that I may broadcast to the nation. Finally, I call upon each and every one of you to exert himself to the utmost so that we may meet the trying days which lie ahead. (reconstructed in Butow, 1954: 208)

The Emperor's speech was followed by a meeting of the Cabinet, which unanimously endorsed the imperial decision. The next day, inside Studio Eight of Japan's National Broadcasting Company, Announcer Wada Chokugen took up the same microphone over which nearly four years earlier he had announced the bombing of Pearl Harbor. At exactly noon he spoke: 'This will be a broadcast of the gravest importance. Will all listeners please rise. His Majesty the Emperor will now read his imperial rescript to the people of Japan. We respectfully transmit his voice' (quoted in Toland, 1970: 850). For the first time ever, the Emperor of Japan directly addressèd his subjects.[6] Over the static of the radio, in a high-pitched, nasal voice, and in a language so formal as to be almost unintelligible to the average Japanese, the Emperor asked his people to 'endure the unendurable' and accept defeat in war.

NOTES

[1] There is some question as to whether by this the United States also meant a Japanese withdrawal from Manchuria. See Toland, 1970: 145.

[2] The orders indicated that the force would be instructed to return to Japan if any agreement were forthcoming between 26 November and 7 December.

[3] Respectively, Suzuki Kantaro, Togo Shigenori, Anami Korechika, Yonai Mitsumasa, Umezu Yoshijiro, and Oikawa Koshiro.

[4] It is estimated that the blast killed 70,000, and injured 60,000 (Hane, 1992: 337).

[5] Butow notes that there is no transcript of the Emperor's exact remarks and that this text 'is based primarily on the accounts subsequently written by persons who attended the imperial conference.'

[6] A group of extremists in the military began planning a coup on 11 August, believing they were acting in accordance with the 'true will' of the Emperor. They planned to wrest all control from the civilian government, put the Emperor under their protection, and continue to prosecute the war. The coup failed when the conspirators were unable to locate the record containing the Emperor's radio broadcast announcing the surrender.

CHAPTER SEVEN

THE ALLIED OCCUPATION

For the vast majority of the Japanese, kept in the dark about the progress of the war, the Emperor's radio broadcast on 15 August came as a 'bolt from the blue' (Shigemitsu, 1958: 366), and some, especially in the military, responded to the news by committing suicide. Most Japanese, however, welcomed the surrender as an unexpected end to the horror of war, reacting with grateful disbelief to their reprieve from 'utter devastation.' As former US Ambassador to Japan Edwin O. Reischauer (1988: 103) wrote, 'The leaders had expected to win through the superiority of Japanese will power, and the people had responded with every ounce of will they possessed, until they were spiritually drained. Not just the cities, but the hearts of the people had been burned out.' From the outbreak of the China Incident in 1937 to the end of the Pacific War in 1945, 2.1 million Japanese soldiers and civilians died in the war and millions of others were wounded and sickened, out of a population that had numbered some 73 million people in 1940. Physically as well, Japan was in ruin. Tokyo and Osaka lost about 60 percent of their dwellings, and nationally, 8 million Japanese were homeless. Japan's economy was near collapse, with 1945 industrial output hovering at 10 percent of prewar levels. Most seriously, Japan faced a severe food shortage, with each person receiving a mere 1,050 calories per day, 500 calories less than subsistence (Hane, 1996: 12).

For the first time in their history, the Japanese also faced the uncertainty of foreign occupation. The Allied Occupation, while formally under the direction of the 11-nation Far Eastern Commission, was in fact almost totally in American hands. This in turn meant that the Occupation was also dominated by the imposing General Douglas MacArthur, who as Supreme Commander of the Allied Powers (SCAP) had broad authority in directing its course. One Japanese man likened MacArthur to 'the wind that blows, the river that flows,' and the Japanese people, already conditioned to follow authority, readily accepted MacArthur's dictation. 'While many Japanese,' wrote George Atcheson in a political dispatch to President Truman in early November 1945, 'are still bewildered and apathetic, what resentment they feel is rather toward their own poor government and inept officials rather than toward us. Most ... are ... generally in a mood for reform and change' (quoted in Livingston et al., 1973: 12).

Reform and change is exactly what the Occupation brought. Recognizing that the vindictive peace imposed on the vanquished after World War I had only fueled further conflict, Americans determined to follow a constructive policy to rebuild Japan into a peace-loving country that would not pose a threat in the future. This meant that the country must be demilitarized. The Americans believed that militarism was imposed on Japan by despotic rulers, and that no free people would of their own accord choose the course of military aggression. Thus, the surest path to demilitarization was through democratization. Demilitarization and democratization were SCAP's two interdependent goals in the Occupation of Japan.

The Allied Occupation lasted over six years, much longer than the originally planned three years. During this time the goals of demilitarization and democratization were to be achieved through reforms based on an American model. Firm in the belief that American society offered the best way of life, SCAP also believed American values could be universally applied. The Occupation of Japan constituted an attempt to rework Japan in fundamental ways, and indeed during the Occupation Japan underwent a period of change unrivalled since the days of Meiji. During the Meiji period, the West had served as a catalyst for change and reform that was directed from within. Under the Occupation, SCAP provided the catalyst and direction for change. Had that direction not been compatible with Japan's own goals and desires, however, the major changes wrought by the Occupation could never have occurred. The respected Japanese historian Irokawa Daikichi (1995: 39) writes:

> It cannot be said that the United States reformed Japan. GHQ [SCAP General Headquarters] simply provided Japan with the opportunity to carry out reforms. Their gift was the destruction of the obstacles that had stood in the way of reform. The Japanese people have not forgotten this great accomplishment. But the people who gave substance to the reform measures and turned them into reality were the reformers among the Japanese people – not the occupation authorities or the conservative government. They were, instead, those who experienced the terrible wartime and postwar crucible and developed a powerful will to endure and live, survived the ordeals, and worked strenuously for the revival of Japan.

In the international climate that developed in the aftermath of the war, with the rise of communism on the Asian continent and the expansion of Soviet power in central Europe, the United States began to look to Japan as a potential ally. While original Occupation intentions were to build Japan as a peaceful, relatively weak agrarian nation with a series of reforms inspired by New Deal thinking, the success of the communist revolution in China prompted Occupation policy to undergo a 'reverse course.' After early 1948, the Occupation shifted its focus to building Japan into an economic powerhouse that would serve as a bulwark against communism in East Asia. When Japan signed the San Francisco Peace Treaty in April 1952, ending the Occupation, it also signed the United States–Japan Mutual Security Treaty with the United States. Seen as a necessary protection for Japan, which had renounced the use of military force in its postwar constitution, this treaty tied Japan and the United States together and also enabled Japan to focus on the economic development that has been the hallmark of its postwar experience.

FIRST STEPS

As the war was ending, US Secretary of State James F. Byrnes was already laying the groundwork for Occupation plans in Japan: 'The ultimate form of government of Japan,' he wrote, 'shall ... be established by the freely expressed will of the Japanese people' (quoted in Butow, 1954: 245). Among the first steps in this direction was the Allied decision to retain the Emperor. Many in the United States felt Hirohito should be deposed and tried as a war criminal, and apparently Hirohito himself was willing to abdicate the throne to accept responsibility for Japan's aggression. But at the urging of MacArthur and prewar US Ambassador to Japan Joseph Grew, the Emperor was kept as a rallying figure to help lead the Japanese through the many changes of the Occupation. Two days after the surrender, the Emperor appointed a new Cabinet to replace the Suzuki Cabinet. At its head was Prince Higashikuni Naruhiko (1887–1990). Japanese governmental leaders believed that Higashikuni's status as a member of the imperial family would help smooth over any lingering opposition to peace.

The first occupying forces arrived in Japan on 28 August 1945, accompanied by journalists from all around the world. Days later, MacArthur arrived in Yokohama to prepare for the signing of the instrument of surrender. For the Japanese government, the impending ceremony caused consternation. Who would represent the Emperor? When others shied away from the onerous task, Foreign Minister Shigemitsu stepped forward to accept the burden. He later wrote:

> I myself had longed with all my soul for the end of the war and, behold, it had come to pass. It was my duty to carry through the last decisive act. I summoned all my resolution and determined to set the final seal on my services to the Throne. For all I knew, a bomb might be my reward, but that counted for little. I hoped and prayed that surrender was to be the dawn of a brighter era in which Japan might live. (1958: 372)

On the decks of the battleship *Missouri*, on 2 September, Shigemitsu and Chief of the General Staff General Umezu Yoshijiro signed the document, followed by MacArthur, and representatives of the other Allied powers.

DEMILITARIZATION

The first task facing the occupying forces was to dismantle Japan's huge war machine. This meant demobilizing Japan's forces, over five million troops and over three million civilians, spread throughout China, Korea and Southeast Asia. In one of his first acts as Prime Minister, Higashikuni on 17 August dispatched a mission to Manila to arrange the details of the surrender of Japan's troops in China, Manchuria, northern Korea and northern Indochina. One fear was that Japanese soldiers would refuse to surrender; every effort was made to ensure that all troops heard the Emperor's own words commanding them to put down their arms. Lieutenant Onoda, who hid in the Philippine jungles for 29 years unaware of Japan's surrender, is testament to the soldiers' fanatic commitment to the Emperor's cause.

Handling this surrender was a terrifically time-consuming task that took over two years; even then, hundreds of thousands remained as Soviet prisoners in Siberia. The demobilization process was made especially difficult by the food shortage in Japan. Any sudden influx of returned soldiers would add stress to an already precarious situation. Munitions factories were closed down as well. But because by the end of the war nearly every Japanese factory was involved in some way in the manufacture of munitions, this dealt a serious blow to the little that remained of Japanese industry, and thousands lost their livelihood.

More serious than the physical manifestations of militarism was the personnel problem. To avoid the imposition of military government, MacArthur had determined to administer the Occupation through the Japanese government and the Diet. But in order to do this it was necessary to find personnel not tainted by their association with wartime militarism. Occupation authorities forced the Higashikuni Cabinet to resign in October 1945, pointing out that it contained war criminals and had dragged its feet in complying with Occupation directives. In early 1946, SCAP ordered a sweeping purge: anyone deemed to have played a part in Japan's military aggression was prohibited from having an active role in public life. Over 200,000 people were targeted, including government officials, military and police officers, business leaders, journalists, members of ultra-nationalist organizations and even teachers. Approaching the personnel problem from another angle, SCAP dismantled the secret police and released some 2,500 political prisoners, many of them communists. Occupation authorities also demanded the rescission of the Peace Preservation Law, which had provided the legal justification for the repression and imprisonment of thousands during the prewar and war years.

A more delicate task than weeding out militarists from the rank and file was dealing with the issue of war criminals in the ranks of officialdom.

Within days of his arrival in Japan, MacArthur ordered the first round of 40 individuals arrested for war crimes. Trial proceedings were conducted by the International Military Tribunal for the Far East, composed of 11 judges, one each from Australia, Canada, China, France, Great Britain, India, the Netherlands, New Zealand, the Philippines, the Soviet Union and the United States. Over the course of the trials, which opened on 3 May 1946, between 5,500 and 6,000 people were tried for war crimes. Most of these were class 'B' criminals, accused of commanding their troops to commit atrocities, or class 'C' criminals, accused of committing 'minor' atrocities or of mistreating war prisoners. Of these, most were sentenced to prison and over 930 were executed (Hane, 1996: 19–20).

Twenty-eight men were brought to trial as class 'A' war criminals, accused of planning and waging Japan's aggression from 1928 to 1945. Former Prime Minister Prince Konoe committed suicide in December 1945 when he learned that he was to be arrested for war crimes. Three of those originally charged did not stand trial, including wartime Foreign Minister Matsuoka Yosuke, responsible for the Tripartite Pact, who died during the trial, as did Admiral Nagano Osami. Ultra-nationalist leader Okawa Shumei went insane and was declared unfit for trial. When the trials ended two and a half years after they began, 25 of the original 28 were found guilty. Former Prime Minister Tojo, who had failed in a suicide attempt shortly before his arrest in September 1945 (he had asked a doctor to mark the location of his heart on his chest and had shot himself), was convicted to death by hanging. Six others, including one civilian, Hirota Koki, Foreign Minister at the time of the Rape of Nanking in 1937, met the same fate. Sixteen were sentenced to life in prison. Former Foreign Minister Togo Shigenori was sentenced to 20 years in prison, and former Foreign Minister Shigemitsu Mamoru, signer of the instrument of surrender, was sentenced to seven years in prison (Hane, 1996: 15–16). In the ongoing controversy about Japan's failure to own adequately its responsibility for the war, it is interesting to note that unlike Germany, Japan did not conduct war trials on its own initiative.

A problematic issue surrounding the question of war responsibility is the Emperor's own personal role. In concert with the decision to retain the Emperor as a rallying point for the Japanese people came the decision not to try Hirohito for war crimes. Until the Showa Emperor's death in January 1989, his responsibility for the war was rarely discussed openly. But in a singularly poignant 1988 statement about Japan's war effort, ex-soldier Ogawa Tamotsu alluded to the question:

> I don't hate Americans now. I don't bear a grudge against anyone with the exception of one person. I cannot speak his name aloud. That person is still alive. He had an excellent education and was able to judge for himself.

> He was in a position to stop the war at the Imperial Conferences. I don't care what other people say. He cannot avoid the responsibilities of war. (quoted in Cook and Cook, 1992: 281)

It seems safe to say, however, that the fact that questions of the Emperor's wartime responsibilities were never addressed served as an obstacle to open discussion of war responsibility in the larger society as well. This remains a burden for Japan and a source of criticism from the international community.

Emperor Hirohito himself apparently adhered to the 'emperor organ theory' which was widely accepted by scholars and politicians during the Taisho era, when Hirohito became regent to his father. The theory, espoused most famously by Tokyo Imperial University law professor Minobe Tatsukichi (who was dismissed from his post for *lèse-majesté* for developing the view), held that the sovereignty rested in the state, not the Emperor. Thus, Hirohito apparently viewed his own role as being circumscribed by the Constitution and believed he was therefore required to accept the decisions of the government regardless of his own beliefs. According to his own interpretation of his actions, then, Hirohito was bound by the government's decision to go to war in 1941 and he made the decision to end the war only to break a deadlock when government officials could not themselves agree on whether to accept the Potsdam Declaration. Nevertheless, as Hane (1996: 19) points out,

> regardless of whether Emperor Hirohito played an active role in the decisions that led to aggression and war in Asia and the Pacific region, he was the head of state … War was declared in his name, hundreds of thousands of Japanese soldiers and sailors died in the belief that they were fulfilling his wishes, and millions of Chinese and other people were killed in his name.

POLITICAL REFORM

The cornerstone of political democratization was the new constitution. With great fanfare, on 6 March 1946, MacArthur (1946: 132) announced

> a decision of the emperor and government of Japan to submit to the Japanese people a new and enlightened constitution which has my full approval. This instrument has been drafted after painstaking investigation and frequent conference between members of the Japanese government and this headquarters following my initial direction to the cabinet five months ago.

In fact, however, MacArthur's announcement glossed over the reality that the new constitution had been written wholly by the Americans.

The Higashikuni Cabinet had been replaced by a cabinet formed by Shidehara Kijuro, the prewar Foreign Minister. In this capacity, Shidehara assembled a committee of legal scholars and others to oversee the drafting of a new constitution, convened in early 1946. But SCAP rejected their draft as too conservative and, with sovereignty still residing in the Emperor, too similar to the problematic Meiji Constitution. MacArthur then instructed General Courtney Whitney, chief of SCAP's Government Section, to draft a new constitution for Japan. Thus, in February 1946, Whitney gathered his staff together and proclaimed them a constitutional assembly. With one week to complete the job, they were guided by MacArthur's instructions that the new document must vest sovereignty not in the Emperor but in the Japanese people and that in it 'Japan was to renounce war forever, abolish her armed forces, and pledge never to revive them' (Gayn, 1973: 20).

By 19 February, Whitney was ready to present the new document for the Japanese government's review. Leaving the draft (in English) with Prime Minister Shidehara, Foreign Minster Yoshida Shigeru (who would later serve as Prime Minister for most of the period 1946–1954) and a few others, Whitney informed them they would have 15 minutes to look over the document. Their 15 minutes up, the flabbergasted Japanese officials were told 'If you are not prepared to sponsor a document of this type, General MacArthur will go over your heads to the Japanese people. But if you will support a constitution of this kind, General MacArthur will support you' (quoted in Gayn, 1973: 22). Despite MacArthur's posturing, most Japanese recognized the foreign origins of the Constitution: having been asked by an American reporter what he thought of the new Constitution, one Japanese reportedly replied, 'Oh, has it been translated into Japanese?' (Duus, 1976: 243). After it was translated into Japanese, the Diet then deliberated, adopting the new Constitution on 29 August 1946. Though Japan's postwar Constitution was hardly written in keeping with Secretary of State Byrnes's promise of a government 'established by the freely expressed will of the Japanese people,' it has remained unamended since it went into effect over half a century ago.

The central change of the 1947 Constitution (so called because it went into effect 3 May 1947) was to place sovereignty in the people and reduce the Emperor to a constitutional monarch, a 'symbol of the state and of the unity of the people.' Henceforth his only role would be ceremonial, as defined by the Cabinet. The wealth and assets of the imperial family were transferred to the national treasury and they became dependent for their livelihood on appropriations subject to annual Diet confirmation. In preparation for this new status, on New Year's Day 1946 the Emperor renounced his divinity with a 'declaration of humanity' that was published in newspapers across the nation. He subsequently made himself more visible among the people, looking very human indeed at just over five feet tall and dressed in rumpled raincoat and fedora.

With sovereignty vested in the people, the 1947 Constitution also wrought major changes in the Diet, which now controls the budget and all the prerogatives previously belonging to the Emperor. The Cabinet, which in the prewar system had stood independent of Diet control, was made responsible to the Diet, as in the British system: the Prime Minister is the president of the majority party in the lower house. The new Constitution also abolished non-parliamentary institutions from the prewar period such as the Privy Council and the military high command. The prewar House of Peers, an appointive body, was changed to the House of Councillors whose members are elected by universal suffrage to six-year terms. Members of the lower house, the House of Representatives, are elected to four-year terms. The lower house has legislative superiority, and can override upper house decisions by a two-thirds majority. The Constitution also established an independent judiciary with a supreme court, charged with judging the constitutionality of all laws. This is one purely American element in a political structure that in most other respects models the British system.

The Constitution protects basic human rights including freedom of speech, the press, assembly, religion, indeed all the rights spelled out in the American Bill of Rights. (MacArthur had earlier dismantled State Shinto and severed all government support for Shinto shrines and activities. Along with this, the imperial nobility was eliminated.) In a radical move for 1946, women were granted equal rights, which paved the way for the abolition of the repressive family system. Going beyond the rights protected by the American Constitution, however, and showing the basic New Deal orientation of the early Occupation period, the 1947 Constitution guaranteed the right to collective bargaining. The Constitution also declared that 'the State shall use its endeavors for the promotion and extension of social welfare and security, and of public health' (quoted in Hane, 1996: 32).

The most dramatic element in the 1947 Constitution, and the most significant in terms of Japan's international role, is the 'Peace Clause,' Article 9, which renounces war as an instrument of the nation. 'Aspiring sincerely to an international peace based on justice and order, the Japanese people forever renounce war as a sovereign right of the nation and the threat or use of force as a means of settling international disputes.' For this reason, the Article continues, 'land, sea and air forces ... will never be maintained. The right of belligerency of the State will not be recognized' (quoted in Lu, 1975: 194). This unique and controversial provision is said to have come directly from MacArthur himself.

SOCIAL REFORM

The Constitution provided the legal setting for fundamental social reforms that would foster the democratization of Japanese society. Chief among these reforms was the complete revision of the civil code in 1948. The prewar 'family system' had prescribed a paternalistic, hierarchical social order. The father's authority in the family was analogous to the Emperor's authority on a national scale. As defined in the 1898 Meiji civil code, the father (or in the absence of the father, the family's eldest son) had 'full control over all family property, the right to determine the family members' place of residence, and the right to approve or disapprove marriages and divorces' (Hane, 1982: 69). Under the new civil code women gained the right to free choice of spouse and of where to live. They had the right to initiate divorce and could own and inherit property in their own names. In the case of divorce where children were involved, the old system had automatically given children into the custody of the father; under the new civil code, the parents would have equal rights in child custody cases. Despite these many legal changes, however, women's place in Japanese society today remains very circumscribed by traditional expectations and social conventions.

Targeting militarism on a broad level and hoping to foster a more democratic outlook among the population, SCAP aimed numerous reforms at education. The prewar system had stressed ethics and morality, with the 1890 Imperial Rescript on Education serving as a cornerstone to inculcate the pupils' loyalty and devotion to the Emperor. Though Ministry of Education bureaucrats opposed SCAP's decision to eliminate the Imperial Rescript on Education, and indeed believed that amid the uncertainty of postwar Japan textbooks should 'defend and promote the mythic imperial polity (*kokutai*) and high moral education' (Hane, 1996: 29–30), MacArthur insisted that education must promote democratic values and individual rights. In the first steps in this direction, schoolchildren sat at their desks, textbooks open before them and inkbrushes ready, crossing out lines of information now deemed untrue or inappropriate, former articles of faith suddenly become false.

Attempting to broaden not only the content but also the accessibility of education, SCAP restructured the school system. The Basic Law on Education, passed in 1947, extended compulsory education to nine years from six years in the prewar period and created a 6–3–3–4 system based on the American model (six years of elementary education, followed by junior and senior high and four years of college). The law also decentralized control over the education system, ending the Ministry of Education's grip on education and placing control in the hands of locally elected school boards. Access to higher education was vastly increased with the opening of 68 new national universities and 99 new regional universities. In the early 1950s this effort was expanded again with the opening of over 200 junior colleges.

ECONOMIC REFORM

Economic reforms would be an important element in the Occupation's effort to reshape Japan. Occupation authorities believed that the causes of the war lay in the collusion of big business and government. A primary ingredient in bringing democracy to Japan would be to foster economic equality. Naturally, the war itself and the destruction it wrought played a major role in economic leveling. But beyond this, the Occupation authorities initially focused on land reform as the center of their economic program. During the prewar period and up to the end of the war, rural poverty had been a serious social and economic problem. By 1945, 70 percent of farm families were either outright tenants, or rented smaller portions of land to supplement their own holdings; nearly half the land under cultivation was rented out (Hane, 1996: 27). Plans for land reform had been floated by the Japanese government in the prewar period, but never implemented. The Occupation offered an opportunity to carry forward ideas already discussed by Japanese leaders, albeit the final policy reached beyond what Japanese officials had originally anticipated.

The Farm Land Reform Law was issued in October 1946. The law outlawed absentee landlordism. Landowners could rent out a limit of 2.5 acres, and only if they lived in the community where they rented out the land. Farmers could own no more than 7.5 acres of farmland, and 2.5 acres of non-farmland. The government purchased all land in excess of these figures and sold it to the cultivators on easy terms: 3.2 percent interest over 30 years. Those whose land was purchased, on the other hand, did not fare as well. By 1947–49, when most of the land purchasing by the government was finalized, skyrocketing inflation 'had reduced the real value of the transaction price to only 1 percent of prewar land prices' (Patrick, 1970: 302). Inevitably, many landlords resisted or tried to resist the law. The chaos and confusion of the immediate postwar period on the one hand made the land reform more difficult, but it was also a time when, as Ronald Dore (1973: 189) has written, 'people were sufficiently bewildered and ready for change to make such a drastic measure possible.' By 1950, tenancy rates had been reduced to about 10 percent, and the land reform is widely regarded as the most successful of the Occupation reforms.

A more troubling economic reform was the effort to break up the *zaibatsu*, the huge financial combines whose grip on the economy and links with the government were believed to have fueled Japanese military aggression. Here, too, the Occupation belief was that breaking up monopolistic enterprises and thus 'spreading the wealth' would serve to foster greater democracy. During the last half of 1945, SCAP froze all *zaibatsu* capital. In 1947, the Anti-Monopoly Law outlawed *zaibatsu* holding companies and *zaibatsu* stock was sold to the public. Under the Deconcentration Law of

1947, 325 companies were designated to be split into their constituent companies. These measures provoked alarm in Japan and among the American right, and in 1949 'it became clear that further surgery to improve the Japanese economy for social and political reasons might kill it instead' (Reischauer, 1988: 107). The Deconcentration Review Board eventually singled out only 19 companies for actual reorganization.

Another major focus for democratization via economic reform was the industrial labor force. Prior to the war, only 8 percent of industrial workers belonged to labor unions, and even this small movement was quashed in 1940 when the Greater Japan Industrial Patriotic Association was organized to promote the nation's war aims. In late 1945, the Diet passed legislation guaranteeing the right to organize, to strike and to bargain collectively. Some 18 months later the Diet passed the Labor Standards Act, which regulated working hours, provided for workers' compensation, established safety and sanitation standards, and placed limits on child labor. After the passage of these bills, labor unionization grew rapidly, embracing some 40 percent of the industrial work force, organized in 35,000 separate unions.

REVERSE COURSE

The first two years of the Occupation thus saw the passage of a plethora of democratizing reforms based on a vision of Japan as a stable, but militarily weak agrarian nation. This vision of Japan's future began to change subtly in 1947 as the Cold War got under way, and the rise of the Chinese Communist Party on the continent and the Truman Doctrine of containment began to create the 'new world order' of the postwar years. In light of the emerging geopolitical situation, Occupation authorities and the Japanese government as well began to shift toward building Japan into a strong Asian ally against the spread of communism.

The first indications of this 'Reverse Course' in Occupation policy came in February 1947, when the conservative Prime Minister Yoshida Shigeru announced that workers who took part in a planned general strike would not be paid. Yoshida, who would lead the country as premier in five separate cabinets between 1946 and 1954, was a conservative politician who had begun his career as a foreign service officer. His imprisonment by Tojo during the war for promoting a peace plan and his reputation as a liberal friend of the United States and Great Britain (having served as Ambassador to Britain in 1936–1938) provided him with strong credentials in the postwar political world. Most of the early Occupation reforms were implemented during the Shidehara Cabinet (October 1945 – May 1946) and the first Yoshida Cabinet (May 1946 – May 1947). But when Yoshida regained the premiership in October 1948, he promoted an increasingly conservative agenda, signs of which had been evident in his response to the planned general strike of early 1947. SCAP, which had previously been a vigorous promoter of labor causes, backed Yoshida's strike ban when MacArthur himself formally issued an order banning the strike.

The growing red scare also heightened concern over Japan's sluggish economic recovery and growth. Focusing attention on this problem, SCAP brought conservative American banker Joseph Dodge to Japan in early 1949. Prior to his departure for Japan, Dodge received a briefing from President Truman in which Truman indicated that the 'National Security Council considered the Japanese economy as one of the most important international issues it had to face at that time' (Kolko and Kolko, 1973: 134). In Japan Dodge presented the nine-point plan he had developed in the six months prior to his arrival. The austerity measures, including balancing the budget, wage and price controls, credit restrictions and tax reform, were socially unpopular and provided the impetus for widespread demonstrations promoted by the Japanese Communist Party. This resulted in a crackdown on the communist movement in Japan, with MacArthur even suggesting that the party be made illegal. Although this did not happen, Yoshida instituted a purge of communists in both government service and private industry which began just prior to the outbreak of the Korean War.

North Korea's invasion of South Korea on 25 June, 1950 provided further impetus for the Occupation's Reverse Course. Shortly after the outbreak of this first instance of actual fighting in the Cold War, MacArthur authorized the formation of a 75,000 member self-defense force to compensate for the American forces that left Japan for Korea. Because of the constitutional prohibition on maintaining 'war potential,' this force was called the National Police Reserve, with proponents arguing that it was not for military purposes but rather was designed to maintain civil order in Japan. Prime Minister Yoshida, though intent upon signing a peace treaty to end the Occupation and restore Japanese sovereignty, opposed creation of this force on the grounds that it would funnel Japanese funds away from his efforts to promote Japan's economic growth. Confident that his political enemies, the Japanese Socialist Party, would oppose the creation of the force, Yoshida satisfied the American authorities by introducing two bills into the Diet to transform the police force into a self-defense force. Though the Socialists reacted as Yoshida anticipated, the bills nevertheless passed on the strength of other supporters in the Diet and the constitutional problems were smoothed over with a supreme court interpretation of Article 9 that said the Constitution did not prohibit defensive capabilities. In the years since, military expenditures have been informally limited to 1 percent of gross national product. Nevertheless, Japan's current military is one of the largest in the world.

The Korean War not only prompted the creation of Japan's Self-

Defense Force, but it was also the catalyst for Japan's spectacular postwar economic growth. Thus Yoshida's concerns that rearmament costs would hinder economic growth were unfounded. American procurements for various supplies, especially from the steel and other heavy industries, promoted an economic boom in Japan that continued even after the war ended (in a stalemate) in July 1953.

PEACE AND SECURITY

The creation of the Self-Defense Force and the economic boom that accompanied the Korean War also helped spur the movement toward concluding a peace treaty. MacArthur had originally envisioned a short Occupation, and as early as spring 1947 he called for planning on a peace treaty. But it would be another three years before Secretary of State John Foster Dulles was authorized, with the State Department, to begin formal discussions of such a treaty. The outbreak of the Korean War made the rapid end to the Occupation a major concern for the United States, but one of the main sticking points in arranging a peace treaty was the issue of which countries would be represented. Relations with both the Soviet Union and China, two of Japan's wartime enemies, had deteriorated to such a state that their representation at a peace conference was uncertain.

The peace conference convened in September 1951 and the San Francisco Peace Treaty was signed on 8 September by 48 countries, excluding China, the Soviet Union, Poland, and Czechoslovakia. China was not invited to the conference because of disagreement over *which* China – the Peoples' Republic of China or Taiwan – represented the legitimate government of that country. The Soviet Union and its eastern European allies refused to sign the treaty, insisting that 'no real peace' was possible without China. The treaty, which went into effect in April 1952, restored Japanese independence and ended the Occupation. In it, Japan formally renounced all rights and territories it gained through aggression, including Taiwan, Korea, Manchuria and Southeast Asia.

At the same time the peace treaty was signed, the United States and Japan signed the Mutual Security Treaty. Dulles had advocated linking the peace treaty to a security arrangement between the United States and Japan. In light of the constitutional prohibition on Japan's military capabilities, the opening of this American 'military umbrella' over Japan seemed to serve the interests of both nations. The treaty allowed the United States to maintain military bases in Japan and to station troops there. But the Mutual Security Treaty inspired considerable opposition in Japan. The conservative parties generally favored the agreement, believing, like Prime Minister Yoshida, that the arrangement would allow Japan to focus on economic growth. The extreme right as well as the left opposed the treaty because it allowed foreign troops to remain on Japanese soil. The treaty came up for additional criticism because it was signed while Japan was still an occupied nation.

MacArthur, the man most closely identified with the Occupation, was replaced as Supreme Commander for the Allied Powers in April 1951 by General Matthew Ridgeway. Truman dismissed MacArthur over a disagreement about the use of force in Korea. When SCAP left Japan in April 1952, it left a nation transformed. The Occupation goals of democratization and demilitarization had been promoted through a variety of political, social and economic reforms. Many of these reforms were in keeping with democratizing trends already present in Japanese society before the war. Japan had, in the words of the social critic Hasegawa Nyozekan (1945: 2), 'taken advantage of defeat.' The Occupation had been midwife to a new, healthy, postwar Japan.

PART THREE ASSESSMENT

CHAPTER EIGHT

TAKING ADVANTAGE OF DEFEAT: JAPAN IN THE POSTWAR ERA

Since the end of the war and the Occupation, it seems Japan has indeed 'taken advantage of defeat.' In the late 1980s Hatanaka Shigeo, former editor of the leading monthly, *Chuo koron*, who was arrested in 1944 as an alleged communist, spoke of Japan's war and defeat:

> It really was a miserable era. I wish such a period had never existed. But because Japan lost, we are able to speak [freely] like this. This, too, is a paradox. If we'd won, we might have been more miserable. Maybe we should thank America. (quoted in Cook and Cook, 1992: 227)

Japan's quest for international strength began in the late nineteenth century as a response to American demands for treaty relations. When the Tokugawa government proved unequal to the task of leading Japan through this crisis and preserving the country's national independence, a group of young samurai overthrew their government and established the new Meiji government. The twin goals of 'Rich Country, Strong Army' guided these remarkable new leaders as they rebuilt their nation using Western political, economic and military models. Phenomenally successful, within a generation Japan had fought and won wars against both China and Russia, and established colonial control over Taiwan and Korea. But rapid change brought social dislocation, and by the early part of the twentieth century governmental leaders grew concerned that this social dislocation would derail Japan's national progress. Their response was to establish ever-tighter control over the population.

The increasingly chaotic situation in China in the 1910s and early 1920s also contributed to Japanese national insecurities. The Japanese response was to take an aggressive stance toward China, first in the Twenty-One Demands of 1915, and again in 1931 by carving out Manchuria as a Japanese colony. Japan's actions on the continent raised protests from the West and put Japan and the United States on a collision course. The collision occurred at Pearl Harbor in 1941, inaugurating the Pacific War and also bringing the United States into the war in Europe.

When the war ended in 1945, Japan lay in ruin. The Allied Occupation sought to rebuild Japan as a peaceful agrarian nation through a series of reforms designed to demilitarize and democratize the country. With the rise of communism in Asia and the outbreak of the Korean War in 1950, the United States began to view Japan as an Asian bulwark against communism, prompting a new push for industrial growth and 'defensive' military build-up. When the Peace Treaty was signed in 1951, Japan and the United States also signed the Mutual Security Treaty, linking them together militarily and providing for the close, though at times rocky relationship that continues today.

One result of the military alliance between Japan and the US is that it allowed Japan to focus its resources on economic and industrial growth (Johnson, 1982: 3). Japan's postwar economic growth first sparked international attention in 1962 when the London *Economist* published an article entitled 'Consider Japan,' which touted the phenomenal development the nation had achieved since the end of the war. Playing host to the Olympic games in 1964 served as 'official notice' of that development.

JAPAN IN 1952: POSTWAR SOCIETY AND CULTURE

Mikiso Hane (1996: 173) writes that in 1945, 'All the beliefs and values [the Japanese] had been taught since childhood were shattered ... The Japanese people were reduced to ground zero in their moral, intellectual, and spiritual life.' They suffered from what was at the time called the '*kyodatsu* condition,' a state of exhaustion and despair, a 'psychic collapse,' that was deemed '"the great enemy that could destroy Japan"' (Dower, 1999a: 89).

The Imperial broadcast announcing Japan's surrender in mid-August 1945, which the Japanese people greeted with an admixture of stunned grief and unspeakable relief, began the process of dismantling the social and cultural order that had dominated the country in the decades before the war. This was followed just months later, on 1 January 1946, with another major communication, this time printed in the newspapers. The 'Rescript to Promote the National Destiny' was a document in which the Emperor renounced his divinity, deeming false the 'conception that the Emperor is divine and that the Japanese people are superior to other races and fated to rule the world' (quoted in Large, 1992: 147).

Rebuilding the 'moral, intellectual and spiritual life' would take place against a backdrop of a struggle for sheer physical survival. Allied bombing left the cities in rubble, farmland torn up and distribution lines destroyed. Even before Japan's surrender, food had been in such short supply that newspapers had instructed the people to add protein to their diets by consuming such things as worms, snails, rats and mice. 'Eat This Way –

Endless Supplies of Materials by Ingenuity,' read the headlines (Dower, 1999a: 91). Now, Japan's empire, which before the war had supplied major portions of the nation's rice, soy, sugar and salt, was lost. Moreover, millions of able-bodied men were stranded in far-flung reaches of Japan's wartime empire.

Obviously, the first concern for the Japanese and for the Occupation authorities was to stave off starvation, find shelter and somehow maintain civil order among the war-weary population. As these efforts were under way and throughout the Occupation period, a new postwar culture was developing; after nearly seven years of incessant change and rebuilding, when the Occupation forces left in 1952, they left a society and culture that were markedly different from what had existed in the prewar period. If any single term could be used to describe Japan's postwar culture, it would have to be 'middle class.'

Much of this postwar culture was shaped directly by Occupation reforms, but always overlaid on foundations that had been put in place during the Meiji period. Rural Japan, for example, which had been plagued with poverty and tenancy in the decade immediately preceding the war, was vastly changed by the Occupation's land reform program. The Occupation's program of land reform greatly reduced tenancy in the countryside, which in turn reduced the paternalism that had been traditional in Japan's villages. Tenants were no longer beholden to the large landowners. With land ownership significantly equalized, status differences between villagers largely dissolved. Land reform contributed to the creation of a large class of rural landowners, most of whom enjoyed greater productivity and better incomes. Here now was a rural middle class, ready and able to participate in self-government.

These changes in rural Japan helped to ameliorate to some extent the extreme urban–rural split that had characterized Japan in the prewar years. In prewar Japan, the dichotomy between the urban and rural areas had been so pronounced that in 1937 rural Japanese children were on average two centimeters shorter than their urban counterparts. On the other hand, the rural setting during the war meant less deprivation for rural children and they on average suffered less malnutrition than did urban children (Dower, 1999a: 92). Mass communications and improved transportation also helped to erase some of the extremes that divided urban and rural Japanese. The development of a vast network of inter- and intra-urban railways made Japan into a commuter society and contributed to the helter-skelter development of suburban communities. Very often, former rural areas were subsumed by this suburban growth, which often happened so rapidly that they developed at first without a proper urban infrastructure of roads, sewers and schools.

Another Occupation reform that had a significant effect on postwar culture was the revision of the civil code, which went into effect in 1947. Just as land reform served to reduce the rigid social distinctions in rural Japan, the new civil code worked fundamental changes in the Japanese family, freeing women from the straitjacket of traditional male control. Women were guaranteed equal rights in the 1947 Constitution and the new civil code guaranteed the equality of husbands and wives in such things as property rights, inheritance rights, divorce and child custody. Because it made for smaller plots, the land reform contributed to a move away from extended families living together under one roof. Instead, in the postwar period, the trend was toward nuclear families, and women were largely freed from the notorious prewar scourge, the tyrannical live-in mother-in-law. Having been granted the vote for the first time in Japan's history, women made an impressive showing in politics. In the first postwar election in 1946, for example, 13 million women cast their ballots for the first time ever and elected 39 women to the Diet. Though this figure would subsequently decline, and women in the early twenty-first century in Japan hold only about 3 percent of the seats in the Diet (Hane, 1996: 154), the status of Japanese women underwent a sea change over the course of the Occupation.

Urban Japan too experienced vast change in the immediate postwar years, also seeing the growth of a huge middle class. During the war, many people had left the urban areas for the relative safety of the countryside. They returned to the cities gradually, and only when adequate food and shelter became available. The years 1946–48 saw a baby boom, and by the mid-1950s the major urban areas began to experience staggering growth. With the prewar infrastructure reduced to rubble, urban Japan had to be rebuilt. Small dwellings destroyed in the war were replaced by apartment buildings. As had land reform in rural Japan, the appearance of apartment buildings mitigated against multiple generations living together under one roof. In the early postwar years, the urban ideal was the 2DK apartment (two bedrooms, dining room and kitchen), and huge apartment complexes housed the so-called *danchizoku* – the 'apartment tribe' (Duus, 1998: 304).

In 1960 the new Prime Minister, Ikeda Hayato, announced the 'Income Doubling Plan,' his vaunted policy of doubling the average household income over the course of the next ten years. As Peter Duus (1998: 289–90) points out, what sounds like an outrageous goal was in fact quite a safe promise, since between 1954 and 1959 the economy had grown at an annual rate of nearly 11 percent. This kind of growth rate had been evident even earlier, and by the time the Occupation ended in 1952, the nation was experiencing what Japan's new Economic Planning Agency called a 'consumer boom.' As Occupation forces were leaving, food consumption had returned to prewar levels. Household appliances like refrigerators, radios and sewing machines were easily available (Dower, 1999a: 544).

Japan's rapid economic growth was fueled in part by some very traditional aspects of its culture: for example, the Confucian ethic of self-discipline, hard work and frugality. The typical white-collar worker put in nearly 50 hours a week on the job; a six-day work week was the norm, as was overtime. Salaries were funneled into savings accounts, as families saved to buy big-ticket consumer items and also to fund education. Average savings rates of 7 percent in the 1950s climbed as high as 23 percent in the 1970s, providing capital for further economic growth (Duus, 1998: 295).

In the arts, too, Japan has experienced great change. The Occupation period served as a time of transition from the intense government control over artistic expression that characterized the prewar period, to the later postwar artistic milieu whose creativity and exploration has put Japanese design at the forefront of the art world. During the Occupation, the role of art was to support the Allied goals of demilitarization and democratization; this effort was guided by SCAP's Civil Information and Education Section (CIE). Paradoxically, though government censorship was one of the scourges that the Occupation aimed to eradicate, CIE engaged in its own censorship of Japanese art. Film-maker Akira Kurosawa's movie *They Who Step on the Tiger's Tail*, for example, was targeted by both the Japanese government, which during the war banned the piece as too democratic, and by CIE, which found it too feudalistic (Richie, 1997: 19). By and large, however, the sudden end to years of government repression of the arts and artists resulted in an explosion of artistic expression in all areas of the arts.

Film was the area that received the most attention from CIE, and film arguably reached the largest audience in the postwar years. In this, as elsewhere, the effort was to promote the message of democratization. Inspired in part by the American films that flooded Japan right after the war, Japanese film-makers began to experiment and move beyond the rigid restrictions placed on them by their wartime government. As soon as American films arrived, Japanese audiences saw kissing on screen for the first time, and indeed CIE encouraged such scenes as a 'symbol of moral liberation.' Soon, Japanese film-makers were including similarly racy shots in their own productions (Richie, 1997: 19). Since this early blossoming of the Japanese film industry, Japan has contributed some of the world's finest directors, including Akira Kurosawa, Imamura Shohei and Kenzo Mizoguchi. Drama proved as important in postwar culture as film. Traditional styles, like *kabuki*, tended to attract the most CIE attention. Modern drama, meanwhile, was treated to a policy of 'benign neglect.'

Literature similarly blossomed in the postwar period. The Occupation approach toward literature was less focused than the policy on film, with the result that CIE engaged in little literary censorship. A period of frivolous, ephemeral literature, called *ero-guro* ('erotic/grotesque' because it consisted primarily of titillating sexual tales), gave way to the mature works of such writers as Tanizaki Jun'ichiro, Natsume Soseki and Yasunari Kawabata.

The visual arts were an important medium for communication in the immediate postwar period. Poster artists were inundated with work, painting emergency announcements and relief notices. Cultural messages were also conveyed via posters. One poster from this period depicts 'then' and 'now' pictures to instruct the population in the ways of cultural democracy. 'Then' the Emperor stood above all others; 'now' all stand on an equal plane (Dower, 1999a: 368). As Japan moved away from the wartime rigors, visual artists experimented with surrealism and the avant-garde, genres that had previously been censored. Since the Occupation period, Japanese artists have moved forward to develop some of the most highly regarded art in the world.

ASSESSMENT OF WAR ISSUES

In the now over half-century since the end of World War II, two war-related issues in particular continue to inspire controversy among historians and laymen alike. One issue that has received increased attention recently is the question of Emperor Hirohito's war responsibility. Since his death in 1989, scholars both in and outside of Japan have revisited this question, with some surprising new insights. Another issue with global significance is the US decision to use the atomic bombs to end the war. Scholarly views on this question, too, have gone through several permutations in the years since the war.

Perhaps the most famous photograph from the Occupation shows General MacArthur, dressed casually in his khaki uniform, top button open, arms akimbo, standing next to (and towering over) the stiffly formal Emperor Hirohito, clad in a cutaway jacket and high collar. The general interpretation of this photograph, which caused a sensation when it was published in the Japanese newspapers in late September 1945, has been that it shows the immense authority that MacArthur wielded over the intensely uncomfortable Hirohito. In his recently published book, *Embracing Defeat: Japan in the Wake of World War II*, however, historian John Dower (1999a: 277–301) adds a subtle but tremendously important insight: the picture also conveyed the message that MacArthur would stand by and support the Emperor.

The Potsdam Declaration of 26 July 1945 called for Japan's unconditional surrender. That Japan fought on for nearly three more weeks is attributed to the fact that unconditional surrender provided no protection for the Emperor, or even more importantly, the imperial system. When the war ended on 15 August, the fate of the Emperor was undecided, unknown even to SCAP authorities. Around the world, leaders of the Allied nations generally favored the idea of not only dismantling Japan's imperial government, but also of putting Hirohito on trial as a war criminal. Even Joseph

Grew, who as the last prewar US Ambassador to Japan supported keeping the imperial institution, admitted his belief in October 1945 that 'Hirohito will have to go' (quoted in Dower, 1999a: 279). Certainly there was reason to support the idea that both the imperial system and Hirohito himself would 'have to go.' The arguments were compelling: if the Occupation aimed to rebuild Japan as a democratic nation, what would be the use of the imperial system? Indeed, the ultra-nationalism engendered by Japan's emperor system in large part helped fuel the nation's war effort. Moreover, Hirohito himself should be made to bear responsibility for the war. If war ended only after his direct intervention, then how had it begun, how had it been prosecuted?

In fact, these seemingly straightforward questions have never been adequately answered, in large part because so many official documents were destroyed in the days immediately after surrender. With a view to the possibility of war crimes trials, military men and bureaucrats alike destroyed potentially incriminating documents, an activity so extensive, in fact, that it inspired a sardonic joke: even though the fires caused by air raids were out, clouds of smoke still hovered over Tokyo, due to all the documents being burned (Dower, 1999a: 39). Records remaining that might provide insight into Hirohito's behavior during the war are scant; one of the most extensive is Kido Koichi's diary. Kido Koichi served as Lord Keeper of the Privy Seal from 1940 to 1945, and was Hirohito's closest confidant. But Kido's often cryptic diary, combined with the emerging SCAP intention to retain the Emperor in the months following the surrender, made it possible to paint Hirohito as a man who, though he personally desired peace, believed that as a constitutional monarch he was bound to follow the lead of the military and the Cabinet. This situation was exacerbated by the Meiji Constitution's vagueness on the issue of imperial responsibility. On paper, the Emperor was all-powerful, but actual decision-making power lay with the Cabinet and the military. Edwin Reischauer, who has been called 'the leading figure in postwar American studies of Japan' (Pyle, 1996: 213), wrote in 1977 that:

> None of the three modern emperors [the Meiji, Taisho and Showa emperors] made any real effort to assert his own will against the decisions of his ministers. The present emperor is known to have chafed at the actions of the military in his early years and to have attempted to get reconsideration of the steps leading to war, but the only political decision he himself made, though at the urging of his closest advisers, was when his ministers in August 1945 pointedly presented him with a tied vote on surrender and he opted for accepting the Allied ultimatum. (1988: 240)

In late 1988, with the prospect of Hirohito's death looming, the issue of war responsibility burst into the Japanese headlines when Motoshima Hitoshi, the mayor of Nagasaki, made remarks in the media about the

Emperor's war guilt, pointing in particular to the fate Japan suffered from the atomic bombs. 'It is clear from historical records,' Motoshima said, 'that if the Emperor, in response to the reports of his senior statesmen, had resolved to end the war earlier, there would have been no Battle of Okinawa, no nuclear attacks on Hiroshima and Nagasaki' (quoted in Pyle, 1996: 212–13). Such remarks were deeply controversial, and Motoshima was shot by a right-wing nationalist amid public outcry that he retract his statements. Motoshima eventually recovered from the attack, however, and as if to highlight the importance of opening up such issues, he was also re-elected to office.

In his ground-breaking recent research, however, John Dower argues that Hirohito at the very least bore a moral responsibility for the war and that he in fact played a much more direct role in deciding and implementing war policy. For example, Dower cites an October 1945 report by a military attaché to Hirohito's vice chamberlain, Kinoshita Michio, in which the attaché writes, '"it is obvious that, as the ruler, he [the emperor] bears responsibility for the nation's war unless he is a robot."' It is clear from these and other unique communications, argues Dower, that the Emperor 'understood and gave orders for preparations for war, deployment of the fleet, the mission of the fleet, the decision to pull out the fleet if last-minute diplomatic negotiations with the United States succeeded, and the time for beginning hostilities ... [and] he signed the declaration of war with full knowledge of the military's intentions' (Dower, 1999a: 291–2).

Whatever Hirohito's actual role in the war may have been, however, MacArthur made the decision to retain him. In this decision, MacArthur was influenced by work prepared by members of his wartime staff dedicated to analyzing the enemy. Most influential was Bonner F. Fellers, who served as MacArthur's military secretary and chief of psychological-warfare operations. In a document prepared about a year before Japan's surrender, Fellers wrote: 'to dethrone, or hang, the Emperor would cause a tremendous and violent reaction from all Japanese. Hanging of the Emperor to them would be comparable to the crucifixion of Christ to us. All would fight to die like ants.' Instead, Fellers continued, the Emperor should be retained, and 'be made a force for good and peace provided Japan is totally defeated and the military clique destroyed' (quoted in Dower, 1999a: 282–3). In a cable to President Eisenhower in January 1946, MacArthur himself flamboyantly reiterated Fellers' argument: if the Emperor were not retained the nation would undergo 'a tremendous convulsion ... disintegrate ... [and begin] a vendetta for revenge ... whose cycle may well not be complete for centuries if ever.' Such a scenario, MacArthur wrote, would require a million more US troops to control; once the Occupation forces left, he believed, there would likely arise 'some form of intense regimentation probably along communistic line[s]' (quoted in Dower, 1999a: 324–5).

This alarming prospect, of course, was averted. The famous photograph, argues Dower, was the opening salvo of a media and public relations campaign launched by MacArthur, and later joined by other Occupation authorities as well as by Japanese bureaucrats, to 'whitewash' the Emperor and absolve him of any responsibility. As a result of this policy, Dower writes,

> the Americans came close to turning the entire issue of 'war responsibility' into a joke. If the man in whose name imperial Japan had conducted foreign and military policy for twenty years was not held accountable for the initiation or conduct of the war, why should anyone expect ordinary people to dwell on such matters, or to think seriously about their own personal responsibility? (1999a: 28)

Why then, did Hirohito not abdicate? Why did he not take the initiative himself to assume the burden of responsibility, no matter what his actual role may have been? Certainly there is precedent for this type of behavior in Japanese culture. Indeed, many might argue that as the Emperor in whose name millions of Japanese had suffered and died, Hirohito should have committed suicide. Some of the Emperor's closest advisers, among them the former Prime Minister Konoe (who *did* commit suicide) and former Prime Minister Prince Higashikuni vetted the possibility of abdication, their discussion even reaching the newspapers. There may be several reasons why Hirohito ultimately did not abdicate. His eldest son and heir, Akihito, was a mere twelve years old in 1945. Should the Emperor have abdicated, Akihito would have required a regent until he reached his majority. The obvious choices for this position were either of the Emperor's younger brothers, Prince Takamatsu or Prince Mikasa. Both had extremely iconoclastic ideas about the imperial system, however, and presumably Hirohito was not at all sure he could entrust the imperial institution to their hands. Prince Mikasa, for example, made a splash in 1947 when he publicly criticized the pomp and cirumstance surrounding the promulgation of the new Constitution, deriding the ceremonies and the Emperor himself as 'undemocratic' (Dower, 1999a: 401–2).

For his part, Emperor Hirohito apparently took his role as emperor, and the weight of its history, very seriously. It is possible, for example, that despite his 'renunciation of divinity' in January 1946, Hirohito maintained a belief in his descent from the Sun Goddess, Amaterasu, of Japanese myth. As he revealed in a letter to his son written shortly after the surrender, he was devoted to protecting and preserving the three imperial regalia – mirror, sword and jewel – which were believed to have been passed down from the gods and had been enshrined as imperial symbols since ancient times (Dower, 1999a: 290). A full assessment of Hirohito's war responsibility is the task of future generations of historians.

One of the most enduring controversies surrounding the war is the US decision to use its atomic bombs to induce a Japanese surrender. The bombings of Hiroshima on 6 August 1945, and of Nagasaki three days later, had far-reaching repercussions in the modern era. Internationally, these events launched the nuclear age and led to the Cold War arms race between the superpowers. For Japan, the only nation ever to suffer the direct effects of atomic warfare, the bombings have left an indelible political and psychological mark. The controversy revolves around two main questions. Was the use of the atomic bombs necessary, and what were the motives behind the US decision to unleash its atomic arsenal?

Up until the late 1960s, the general view was that Japan's refusal to surrender after the Potsdam Proclamation in July 1945 propelled the United States toward the next phase of military planning. President Truman, having taken office upon Roosevelt's death in April 1945, was faced with choosing between two alternatives: a land invasion, or the atomic bomb. In mid-June 1945 plans for Operation Olympic, which mapped out the strategy for a US land invasion to begin with an attack on Kyushu in November, were completed.

By late June, the Battle of Okinawa was finally over after nearly three months of fighting. It had been a horribly brutal and costly affair, exacting the highest price of any of the World War II campaigns. Japan lost over 110,000 soldiers, the United States over 12,000. More chillingly, tens of thousands of Okinawan civilians were dead. Many took their own lives to avoid being taken prisoner, the result of years of government indoctrination. Based on this type of evidence, Truman and US military planners had every reason to believe the Japanese would resist a land invasion down to the last man, woman and child, and with this in mind they turned to the atomic bomb.

General George Marshall, US Secretary of the Army, and Henry L. Stimson, who had been US Secretary of War, both advised President Truman to use the bomb, estimating that a land invasion would cost anywhere between half a million to a million American lives alone (not to mention Japanese casualties). Once the decision to use the bombs was made, further considerations came into play: should the Japanese government be warned in advance? Should the bombs be used in uninhabited areas? The decision was made to use it against a Japanese city, and a list of 180 possible targets was drawn up. The important factors in determining which city would be targeted were the 'congestion/inflammability' of the target, essentially how easily could the target be torched, whether there was major war industry in the area, and the presence of transportation facilities at the target (Frank, 1999: 150). For these and other reasons, Hiroshima and Nagasaki were chosen.

Stimson would later reflect on the decision: 'No man, in our position and subject to our responsibilities, holding in his hands a weapon of such possibilities for accomplishing this purpose [inducing a Japanese surrender] and saving those lives, could have failed to use it and afterwards looked his countrymen in the face.' Such a course was, he wrote, 'our least abhorrent choice' (quoted in Pyle, 1996: 211). Indeed, points out historian Duus (1998: 246), 'none of the President's closest advisers counseled against it.' Originally designed for use against Germany, the German surrender in May had eliminated that option. The first successful test of an atomic bomb took place in late July. Days later, the first bomb was dropped on Hiroshima; some 100,000 people ultimately died from the bomb and its after-effects. In Nagasaki, 70,000 Japanese lost their lives. Shortly thereafter one more bomb became available, but Truman ordered that it not be used, later writing in his diary that 'the thought of destroying another city was too horrible' (quoted in Pyle, 1996: 210).

The assessment of the use of the atomic bombs has been profoundly colored by politics. By the 1970s, US scholarship was increasingly influenced by both the continuing Cold War and the ordeal of the Vietnam War. The impact of these events led historians to renewed explorations of the atomic bombings of Japan and several arguments critical of the US decision to use the bombs emerged. One group pointed to a Japan that was already virtually broken, providing as evidence the fact that people close to power, such as Prime Minister Suzuki Kantaro, were quietly advocating peace, and seeking mediation from Russia to end the war. In light of these conditions, they asked, what was the necessity of using atomic weaponry? An unlikely hero for these scholars was General Dwight D. Eisenhower, who advocated against using the atomic bomb.

Other revisionist scholars questioned the American insistence on unconditional surrender as being unnecessarily harsh and vindictive. Leon V. Sigal (1988: 93), for example, argued that 'From its informal origins in the hyperbole of US politics, unconditional surrender gradually became more than a propaganda slogan. Through frequent repetition it became policy ... [and] it left Japan in the dark about the consequences of defeat.' Here we get back to the issue of saving the imperial institution, which did indeed prove to be a major obstacle to Japan's surrender. A former US Ambassador to Japan, Joseph Grew, had argued in favor of making it clear to the Japanese government that the imperial institution would not be tampered with, saying that this would not only speed surrender, but would facilitate postwar rebuilding. This is, of course, exactly what happened, but it happened only after Japan submitted to unconditional surrender without clear reassurances about the imperial institution, and only after the terrible bombings.

Still others argue that the use of the atomic bombs was less an end to the Pacific War and more the beginning of the Cold War. The real target, according to this argument, was Stalin; the bombs were a reminder of US military power and were intended to serve as a warning to the mistrusted ally. The use of the bombs against Japan would ensure that the Soviets would be judicious in extending their power in Asia in the aftermath of their declaration of war against Japan.

More recent scholarship has revisited this important question of the use of the atomic bombs (see Frank, 1999; Maddox, 1995). Richard B. Frank's *Downfall: The End of the Imperial Japanese Empire* is the most recent and most complete attempt to date to view the events from the perspective of Japanese and Allied military planners at the time. Frank brings to light recent evidence showing that Japan was not seriously considering surrender in early August 1945; neither the Emperor nor Japanese military leaders were advocating such a move. Indeed, Frank argues, Japan was planning Operation Ketsu-go, the Homeland defense plan. As Okinawa fell, Japanese soldiers were massing in Kyushu, the numbers nearly tripling from 350,000 in June to 900,000 in August, with more, presumably, to be in place by the 1 November invasion date. On 13 August, Vice-Admiral Takijiro Onishi, the creator of the kamikaze effort, made a bold statement declaring that 'If we are prepared to sacrifice twenty million Japanese lives in a special attack [kamikaze] effort, victory will be ours!' (quoted in Frank, 1999: 311). At that time, the United States could expect to be able to field only about 765,000 soldiers, far less than the desirable ratio of attack force to defending force of three to one (Maddox, 1995: 110). In light of these odds, and in light of the Japanese determination to fight, when the Japanese government rejected the Potsdam Proclamation, Truman decided to use the bombs. Frank quotes Prime Minister Suzuki Kantaro on the Japanese government's reaction to the bombs:

> The Supreme War Council ... was making every possible preparation to meet [an American] landing. They proceeded with that plan until the Atomic Bomb was dropped, after which they believed the United States would no longer attempt to land when it had such a superior weapon – that the United States need not land when it had such a weapon; so at that point they decided that it would be best to sue for peace. (1999: ix)

Frank does not in any way discount the 'indiscriminate effects of the atomic bombs that seared, blasted, and irradiated tens of thousands of noncombatants' (1999: xix). He concludes, however, that the bombs were in fact *the* decisive factor in bringing about a Japanese surrender and avoiding the stunning loss of life, both Japanese and American, that would have resulted from continued fire-bombing and from the otherwise inevitable land invasion.

JAPAN'S POSTWAR CHALLENGES

Japan's emergence as an economic powerhouse has highlighted several challenges Japan faces in the twenty-first century. Most difficult, and most public, is the issue of what role Japan will play in the international community. This issue comes directly out of Japan's past: Japan's quest to find its role in the international community is exactly what motivated Japan during the Meiji Restoration and in its aggressive policies in Asia. It has been said that Japan is not quite Asian, not quite Western. As the first Asian nation to modernize successfully, Japan played a unique role in Asia. But by using its strength against its Asian neighbors, Japan incurred their hostility, bitterness and mistrust. Because of this past, and because many Chinese, Koreans and Southeast Asians feel Japan has never adequately expressed remorse for its actions in their countries, Japan often finds itself in a no-win situation. On the one hand, for example, South Korea negotiated for reparation payments from Japan, and in the early 1960s was extended $300 million in reparations and $300 million in loans. On the other hand, Japanese economic penetration into the Asian economies, in the form of loans and trade, is criticized as economic imperialism. Japan has also been criticized for its failure to provide humanitarian aid commensurate with its economic ability. In the 1980s, for example, Japan virtually closed its doors to Vietnamese 'boat people' refugees. In the early 1990s, however, Japan stepped up its financial commitments to international humanitarian aid, contributing nearly $11 million to developing countries, exceeding US contributions by over $1 million (Hane, 1996: 93).

The phrase 'once burned, twice shy' aptly describes Japan's attitudes toward playing a military role in international events. Not only do memories of wartime suffering make for a nation of pacifists, but Japan's postwar Constitution prohibits Japan from maintaining offensive military capabilities. During the Gulf War in 1990, the United States criticized Japan, which imports over half of its oil from the Gulf States, for not playing a more prominent role in the war against Iraq. The question of whether or not to send Japanese troops abroad was finally resolved by instead sending financial aid, equipment and medical assistance. Japan has also demurred, though not without intense domestic political fights, from sending troops from its Self-Defense Forces to participate in United Nations peace-keeping missions.

The Japanese, too, are leery of any sign of increased governmental power, fearful of a return to the days of the 1930s and early 1940s when the government imposed tight controls over the populace. When the Kobe Earthquake struck in January 1995, for example, the government dragged its feet in sending aid, slow to respond on a national level because of both legal and attitudinal proscriptions on the intrusion of national power at the local level.

Perhaps the international and domestic mistrust of Japanese power originates partly from Japan's failure to examine and address thoroughly its wartime activities. It may be that in order for Japan to find a balanced international role and to secure democracy domestically, it must first seriously address its wartime role in Asia. Questions about war blame and war responsibility were not aired largely due to the immediate postwar decision to retain the Emperor. If Emperor Hirohito were retained, as MacArthur and others decided he must be in order to maintain order in Japan, then he had to be 'sanitized' and in effect divorced from Japan's aggression in Asia. Thus, while other wartime leaders were tried, and some executed, for war crimes, Hirohito was spared trial and his role in carrying out Japan's aggression in Asia was not scrutinized. John Dower (1999b) points to evidence that MacArthur in effect made a subtle 'deal' with Hirohito and the Japanese government: if Hirohito would support Occupation efforts to democratize and demilitarize, he, and more importantly the imperial institution, would be allowed to survive. As a result, Dower argues, there was no real effort to examine fully the issue of war responsibility.

Hirohito died of cancer in 1989, having lived 87 years and served 62 years, the longest life and reign of any emperor in Japanese history. It looked briefly like this would be a time to review and reflect on the past. At a banquet in South Korea shortly after his enthronement, the new Emperor Akihito expressed 'deepest regret for the occupation brought about by my country.' Despite this, and an earlier statement made in 1991 by then Prime Minister Miyazawa Kiichi regarding the 'deep reflection' on the 'unbearable suffering' brought by the war, Japan's Asian neighbors have generally not been satisfied that Japan has engaged in a full reckoning of its wartime responsibilities (Morton, 1994: 251, 247).

The ongoing textbook controversy of recent years reflects Japan's uneasy relationship with its past. In the 1960s, the eminent Japanese historian Ienaga Saburo wrote a history of Japan for high school students. The Ministry of Education, responsible for selecting textbooks for the nation, asked Ienaga to revise strongly worded portions about Japan's wartime past, changing 'invasion' of China into 'advance' into China, and to rewrite portions about the Rape of Nanking and Japanese Army experiments on living Chinese subjects. Ienaga won renown for suing the government for its unconstitutional order to revise the textbooks. The case dragged on for 28 years and was finally settled in 1993 when the Tokyo Higher Court decided that though the Ministry of Education had the right to determine the content of textbooks, it did not have the legal right to order Ienaga to revise his. In short, it was a mixed victory for Ienaga, who said, 'In the end, almost no one wins a lawsuit in Japan against the government. But for more than twenty years I think I have proved a great deal. Even if I couldn't win in court, in the courts of history I think I have been victorious' (quoted in Morton, 1994: 255).

Between 1925 and 1952, Japan experienced great change. In large part because of Japan's actions in Asia, Japan's neighbors also experienced great change. Japanese aggression in China contributed to the rise and ultimate victory of the Chinese Communist Party and the establishment of the People's Republic of China. After years of oppressive Japanese rule, Korea became independent in 1945, only to flounder and split into two harsh and mutually hostile regimes. In Vietnam the French returned to try to erase the humiliation of Japan's take-over of their colony, and for three decades Vietnam engaged in a bloody struggle to establish national independence. Thus, in many ways, Japan and Asia today are products of Japanese actions during the years between 1925 and 1952.

Part of Japan's challenge on the international level will be to find an appropriate role for itself in the community of nations, and especially to work out amicable relations in Asia. On the domestic front, Japan will continue with developments it has struggled with since the Meiji period, the continuing creation of democracy for its citizens. Moving away from the Meiji era emphasis on democracy for the sake of building a strong state, the Japanese people will increasingly move toward democracy on the individual level, with results that will necessarily benefit the state, but more importantly, will provide for the welfare of its people.

PART FOUR   DOCUMENTS

This Meiji Constitution was presented to the Japanese people as a 'gift' from Emperor Mutsuhito and went into effect in February 1890.

Preamble

Having, by virtue of the glories of Our Ancestors, ascended the Throne of a lineal succession unbroken for ages eternal; desiring to promote the welfare of, and to give development to the moral and intellectual faculties of Our beloved subjects, the very same that have been favoured with the benevolent care and affectionate vigilance of Our Ancestors; and hoping to maintain the prosperity of the State, in concert with Our people and with their support, We hereby promulgate, in pursuance of Our Imperial Rescript of the 12th day of the 10th month of the 14th year of Meiji, a fundamental law of the State, to exhibit the principles, by which We are guided in Our conduct, and to point out to what Our descendants and Our subjects and our descendants are forever to conform ...

We now declare to respect and protect the security of the rights and of the property of Our people, and to secure to them the complete enjoyment of the same, within the extent of the provisions of the present Constitution and of the law.

The Imperial Diet shall be convoked for the 23rd year of Meiji and the time of its opening shall be the date, when the present Constitution comes into force.

When in the future it may become necessary to amend any of the provisions of the present Constitution, We or Our successors shall assume the initiative right, and submit a project for the same to the Imperial Diet. The Imperial Diet shall pass its vote upon it, according to the conditions imposed by the present Constitution, and in no otherwise shall Our descendants or Our subjects be permitted to attempt any alteration thereof.

Our Ministers of State, on Our behalf, shall be held responsible for the carrying out of the present Constitution, and Our present and future subjects shall forever assume the duty of allegiance to the present Constitution.

Chapter 1. The Emperor

Article 1. The Empire of Japan shall be reigned over and governed by a line of Emperors unbroken for ages eternal.

Article 2. The Imperial Throne shall be succeeded to by Imperial male descendants, according to the provisions of the Imperial House Law.

Article 3. The Emperor is sacred and inviolable.

Article 4. The Emperor is the head of the Empire, combining in Himself the rights of sovereignty, and exercises them, according to the provisions of the present Constitution.

Article 5. The Emperor exercises the legislative power with the consent of the Imperial Diet.

Article 6. The Emperor gives sanction to laws, and orders them to be promulgated and executed.

Article 7. The Emperor convokes the Imperial Diet, opens, closes, and prorogues it, and dissolves the House of Representatives.

Article 8. The Emperor, in consequence of an urgent necessity to public safety or to avert public calamities, issues, when the Imperial Diet is not sitting, Imperial Ordinances in the place of law.

(2) Such Imperial Ordinances are to be laid before the Imperial Diet at its next session, and when the Diet does not approve the said Ordinances, the Government shall declare them to be invalid for the future.

Article 9. The Emperor issues or causes to be issued, the Ordinances necessary for the carrying out of the laws, or for the maintenance of the public peace and order, and for the promotion of the welfare of the subjects. But no Ordinance shall in any way alter any of the existing laws.

Article 10. The Emperor determines the organization of the different branches of the administration, and salaries of all civil and military officers, and appoints and dismisses the same. Exceptions especially provided for in the present Constitution or in other laws, shall be in accordance with the respective provisions (bearing thereon).

Article 11. The Emperor has the supreme command of the Army and Navy.

Article 12. The Emperor determines the organization and peace standing of the Army and Navy.

Article 13. The Emperor declares war, makes peace, and concludes treaties.

Article 14. The Emperor declares a state of siege.

(2) The conditions and effects of a state of siege shall be determined by law.

Article 15. The Emperor confers titles of nobility, rank, orders and other marks of honor.

Article 16. The Emperor orders amnesty, pardon, commutation of punishments and rehabilitation.

Article 17. A Regency shall be instituted in conformity with the provisions of the Imperial House Law.

(2) The Regent shall exercise the powers appertaining to the Emperor in His name ...

From Ito Hirobumi, *Commentaries on the Constitution of the Empire of Japan*, translated by Miyoji Ito (Tokyo, 1889), pp. xi–32 *passim*.

DOCUMENT 2   THE IMPERIAL RESCRIPT ON EDUCATION, 1889

The Imperial Rescript on Education was issued in conjunction with the Meiji Constitution. Recited daily by schoolchildren throughout the country, this Rescript emphasized traditional Confucian values.

Know ye, Our subjects:

Our Imperial Ancestors have founded Our Empire on a basis broad and everlasting, and have deeply and firmly implanted virtue; Our subjects ever united in loyalty and filial piety have from generation to generation illustrated the beauty thereof. This is the glory of the fundamental character of Our Empire, and herein also lies the source of Our education. Ye, Our subjects, be filial to your parents, affectionate to your brothers and sisters; as husbands and wives be harmonious, as friends true; bear yourselves in modesty and moderation; extend your benevolence to all; pursue learning and cultivate arts, and thereby develop intellectual faculties and perfect moral powers; furthermore, advance public good and promote common interests; always respect the Constitution and observe the laws; should emergency arise, offer yourselves courageously to the State; and thus guard and maintain the prosperity of Our Imperial Throne coeval with heaven and earth. So shall ye not only be Our good and faithful subjects, but render illustrious the best traditions of your forefathers.

The Way here set forth is indeed the teaching bequeathed by Our Imperial Ancestors, to be observed alike by Their Descendants and the subjects, infallible for all ages and true in all places. It is Our wish to lay it to heart in all reverence, in common with you, Our subjects, that we may all attain to the same virtue.

October 30, 1890

Translation from William Theodore de Bary, ed., *Sources of Japanese Tradition* (New York, 1958), pp. 646–7. An early English translation can be found in Dairoku Kikuchi, *Japanese Education* (London, 1909), pp. 2–3.

DOCUMENT 3   KITA IKKI, OUTLINE PLAN FOR THE REORGANIZATION OF JAPAN, 1923

Kita Ikki was an early ultra-nationalist. This 'Outline Plan' emphasized the unique relationship between the Japanese emperor and the Japanese people and called for violent action to restore direct imperial rule. Kita Ikki was executed in 1937 for laying the ideological foundations of the 26 February Incident.

At present the Japanese empire is faced with a national crisis unparalleled in its history; it faces dilemmas at home and abroad. The vast majority of the people feel insecure in their livelihood and they are on the point of taking a lesson from the collapse of European societies, while those who monopolize political, military, and economic power simply hide themselves and, quaking with fear, try to maintain their unjust position. Abroad, neither England, America, Germany, nor Russia has kept its word, and even our neighbor China, which long benefited from the protection we provided through the Russo–Japanese War, not only has failed to repay us but instead despises us. Truly we are a small island, completely isolated in the Eastern Sea. One false step and our nation will again fall into the desperate state of crisis – dilemmas at home and abroad – that marked the period before and after the Meiji Restoration.

The only thing that brightens the picture is the sixty million fellow countrymen with whom we are blessed. The Japanese people must develop a profound awareness of the great cause of national existence and of the people's equal rights, and they need an unerring, discriminating grasp of the complexities of domestic and foreign thought. The Great War in Europe was, like Noah's flood, Heaven's punishment on them for arrogant and rebellious ways. It is of course natural that we cannot look to the Europeans, who are out of their minds because of the great destruction, for a completely detailed set of plans. But in contrast Japan, during those five years of destruction, was blessed with five years of fulfillment. Europe needs to talk about reconstruction, while Japan must move on to reorganization. The entire Japanese people, thinking calmly from this perspective which is the result of Heaven's rewards and punishments, should, in planning how the great Japanese empire should be reorganized, petition for a manifestation of the imperial prerogative establishing 'a national opinion in which no dissenting voice is heard, by the organization of a great union of the Japanese people.' Thus, by homage to the emperor, a basis for national reorganization can be set up.

Section One: The People's Emperor
Suspension of the Constitution. In order for the emperor and the entire Japanese people to establish a secure base for the national reorganization, the emperor will, by a show of his imperial prerogative, suspend the Constitution for a period of three years, dissolve both houses of the Diet, and place the entire nation under martial law.

(Note 1: In extraordinary times the authorities should of course ignore harmful opinions and votes. To regard any sort of constitution or parliament as an absolute authority is to act in direct imitation of the English and American semisacred 'democracy.' Those who do so are the obstinate conservatives who hide the real meaning of 'democracy'; they are as ridiculous as those who try to argue national polity on the basis of the [Shinto mythological] High Plain of Heaven. It cannot be held that in the discussion of plans for naval expansion Admiral Togo's vote was not worth more than the three cast by miserable members of the Diet, or that in voting on social programs a vote by Karl Marx is less just than seven cast by Okura Kihachiro. The effect of government by votes which has prevailed hitherto is really nothing more than a maintenance of the traditional order; it puts absolute emphasis on numbers and ignores those who would put a premium on quality.) ...

The True Significance of the Emperor. The fundamental doctrine of the emperor as representative of the people and as pillar of the nation must be made clear ...

(Note 2: There is no scientific basis whatever for the belief of the democracies that a state which is governed by representatives voted in by the electorate is superior to a state which has a system of government by a particular person. Every nation has its own national spirit and history. It cannot be maintained, as advocates of this theory would have it, that China during the first eight years of the republic was more rational than Belgium, which retained rule by a single person. The 'democracy' of the Americans derives from the very unsophisticated theory of the time which held that society came into being through a voluntary contract based upon the free will of individuals; these people, emigrating from each European country as individuals, established communities and built a country. But their theory of the divine right of voters is a half-witted philosophy which arose in opposition to the theory of the divine right of kings at that time. Now Japan certainly was not founded in this way, and there has never been a period in which Japan was dominated by a half-witted philosophy. Suffice it to say that the system whereby the head of state has to struggle for election by a longwinded self-advertisement and by exposing himself to ridicule like a low-class actor seems a very strange custom to the Japanese people, who have been brought up in the belief that silence is golden and that modesty is a virtue.) ...

The National Reorganization Cabinet. A Reorganization Cabinet will be organized while martial law is in effect; in addition to the present ministries, it will have ministries for industries and several Ministers of State without Portfolio. Members of the Reorganization Cabinet will not be chosen from the present military, bureaucratic, financial, and party cliques, but this task will be given to outstanding individuals selected throughout the whole country ...

The National Reorganization Diet. The National Reorganization Diet, elected in a general election and convened during the period of martial law, will deliberate on measures for reorganization.

The National Reorganization Diet will not have the right to deliberate on the basic policy of national reorganization proclaimed by the emperor. (Note i: Since in this way the people will become the main force and the emperor the commander, this *coup d'état* will not be an abuse of power but the expression of the national determination by the emperor and the people.)

From Ikki Kita, *Nihon Kaizoo Hooan Taikoo* (Tokyo, 1953). This translation from William Theodore de Bary, ed., *Sources of Japanese Tradition* (New York, 1958), pp. 775–83.

DOCUMENT 4   **THE PEACE PRESERVATION LAW, 1925**

The Peace Preservation Law was enacted on 12 May 1925, and was designed to counter-balance the 'rampant democracy' that would be unleashed by the Universal Manhood Suffrage Law enacted the same month.

Article 1. Anyone who has organized an association with the objective of altering the *kokutai* [national polity, *viz.* the emperor system] or the form of government [deleted from the law] or of denying the system of private property, and anyone who has joined such an association with full knowledge of its object, shall be liable to imprisonment with or without hard labor for a term not exceeding ten years.

Any attempt to commit the crime in the preceding clause will also be punished.

Article 2. Anyone who has discussed the execution of matters specified in paragraph 1 of article 1 with the object mentioned therein shall be liable to imprisonment with or without hard labor for a term not exceeding seven years.

Article 3. Anyone who has instigated the execution of matters specified in paragraph 1 of article 1 with the object mentioned therein shall be liable to imprisonment with or without hard labor for a term not exceeding seven years.

Article 4. Anyone who has instigated others to engage in rioting or assault or other crimes inflicting harm on life, person, or property for the purpose of committing those crimes described in paragraph 1 of article 1 shall be liable to imprisonment with or without hard labor for a term not exceeding ten years.

Article 5. Anyone who, aiding others in the commission of those crimes described in paragraph 1 article 1 and in the preceding three articles, provides money, goods, or other financial benefits for others, or makes a proposal or concludes an agreement for the same, shall be liable to imprisonment with or without hard labor for a term not exceeding five years. Anyone who knowingly receives such remuneration, or makes demand or commitment for the same shall be punished in the same manner.

Article 6. Anyone who has committed the crimes described in the five preceding articles and has voluntarily surrendered shall receive reduction of punishment or amnesty.

Article 7. This law shall apply to anyone who violates it even if they are outside its jurisdiction.

Translation from *Kodansha Encyclopedia of Japan* (Tokyo, 1983), VI, p. 168.

DOCUMENT 5   *KOKUTAI NO HONGI (THE FUNDAMENTALS OF OUR NATIONAL POLITY)*, 1937

Kokutai no hongi *was published by the Ministry of Education in 1937 and represented the official governmental interpretation of the emperor system and the relationship between the state and the people.*

Introduction

The various ideological and social evils of present-day Japan are the result of ignoring the fundamental and running after the trivial, of lack of judgment, and a failure to digest things thoroughly; and this is due to the fact that since the days of Meiji so many aspects of European and American culture, systems, and learning, have been imported, and that, too rapidly. As a matter of fact, the foreign ideologies imported into our country are in the main ideologies of the Enlightenment that have come down from the eighteenth century, or extensions of them. The views of the world and of life that form the basis of these ideologies are a rationalism and a positivism, lacking in historical views, which on the one hand lay the highest value on, and assert the liberty and equality of, individuals, and on the other hand lay value on a world by nature abstract, transcending nations and races. Consequently, importance is laid upon human beings and their groupings, who have become isolated from historical entireties, abstract and independent of each other. It is political, social, moral, and pedagogical theories based on such views of the world and of life, that have on the one hand made contributions to the various reforms seen in our country, and on the other have had deep and wide influence on our nation's primary ideology and culture. ...

Paradoxical and extreme conceptions, such as socialism, anarchism, and communism, are all based in the final analysis on individualism, which is the root of modern Occidental ideologies and of which they are no more than varied manifestations. Yet even in the Occident, where individualism has formed the basis of their ideas, when it has come to communism, they have found it unacceptable; so that now they are about to do away with their traditional individualism, and this has led to the rise of totalitarianism and nationalism and to the springing up of Fascism and Nazism. That is, it can be said that both in the Occident and in our country the deadlock of individualism has led alike to a season of ideological and social confusion and crisis. ... This means that the present conflict seen in our people's ideas, the unrest of their modes of life, the confused state of their civilization, can be put right only by a thorough investigation by us of the intrinsic nature of Occidental ideologies and by grasping the true meaning of our national polity. Then, too, this should be done not only for the sake of our nation but for the sake of the entire human race which is struggling to find a way out of the deadlock with which individualism is faced.

Loyalty and Patriotism

Our country is established with the emperor, who is a descendant of Amaterasu Omikami, as her center, and our ancestors as well as we ourselves constantly have beheld in the emperor the fountainhead of her life and activities. For this reason, to serve the emperor and to receive the emperor's great august Will as one's own is the rationale of making our historical 'life' live in the present; and on this is based the morality of the people.

Loyalty means to reverence the emperor as [our] pivot and to follow him implicitly. By implicit obedience is meant casting ourselves aside and serving the emperor intently. To walk this Way of loyalty is the sole Way in which we subjects may 'live,' and the fountainhead of all energy. Hence, offering our lives for the sake of the emperor does not mean so-called self-sacrifice, but the casting aside of our little selves to live under his august grace and the enhancing of the genuine life of the people of a State. The relationship between the emperor and the subjects is not an artificial relationship [which means] bowing down to authority, nor a relationship such as [exists] between master and servant as is seen in feudal morals. ... The ideology which interprets the relationship between the emperor and his subjects as being a reciprocal relationship such as merely [involves] obedience to authority or rights and duties, rests on individualistic ideologies, and is a rationalistic way of thinking that looks on everything as being in equal personal relationships. An individual is an existence belonging to a State and her history which forms the basis of his origin, and is fundamentally one body with it. ...

From the point of individualistic personal relationships, the relationship between sovereign and subject in our country may [perhaps] be looked upon as that between non-personalities. However, this is nothing but an error arising from treating the individual as supreme, from the notion that has individual thoughts for its nucleus, and from personal abstract consciousness. Our relationship between sovereign and subject is by no means a shallow, horizontal relationship such as implies a correlation between ruler and citizen, but is a relationship springing from a basis transcending this correlation, and is that of 'dying to self and returning to [the] One,' in which this basis is not lost. This is a thing that can never be understood from an individualistic way of thinking. In our country, this great Way has seen a natural development since the founding of the nation, and the most basic thing that has manifested itself as regards the subjects is in short this Way of loyalty.

Filial Piety
In our country filial piety is a Way of the highest importance. Filial piety originates with one's family as its basis, and in its larger sense has the nation for its foundation. Filial piety directly has for its object one's parents, but in its relationship toward the emperor finds a place within loyalty ...

Loyalty and Filial Piety as One
Filial piety in our country has its true characteristics in its perfect conformity with our national polity by heightening still further the relationship between morality and nature. Our country is a great family nation, and the Imperial Household is the head family of the subjects and the nucleus of national life. ...

Harmony
When we trace the marks of the facts of the founding of our country and the progress of our history, what we always find there is the spirit of harmony ...

Harmony as in our nation is a great harmony of individuals who, by giving play to their individual differences, and through difficulties, toil and labor, converge as one. Because of individual differences and difficulties, this harmony becomes all the greater and its substance rich. Again, in this way individualities are developed, special traits become beautiful, and at the same time they even enhance the development and well-being of the whole.

Self-Effacement and Assimilation
A pure, cloudless heart is a heart which, dying to one's ego and one's own ends, finds life in fundamentals and the true Way. That means, it is a heart that lives in the Way of unity between the Sovereign and his subjects, a Way that has come down to us ever since the founding of the empire. It is herein that there springs up a frame of mind, unclouded and right, that bids farewell to unwholesome self-interest. The spirit that sacrifices self and seeks life at the very fountainhead of things manifests itself eventually as patriotism and as a heart that casts self aside in order to serve the State. ...

Bushido [The Way of the Warrior]
Bushido may be cited as showing an outstanding characteristic of our national morality. In the world of warriors one sees inherited the totalitarian structure and spirit of the ancient clans peculiar to our nation. Hence, though the teachings of Confucianism and Buddhism have been followed, these have been transcended. That is to say, though a sense of obligation

binds master and servant, this has developed into a spirit of self-effacement and of meeting death with a perfect calmness. In this, it was not that death was made light of so much as that man tempered himself to death and in a true sense regarded it with esteem. In effect, man tried to fulfill true life by way of death. . . .

The warrior's aim should be, in ordinary times, to foster a spirit of reverence for the deities and his own ancestors in keeping with his family tradition; to train himself to be ready to cope with emergencies at all times; to clothe himself with wisdom, benevolence, and valor; to understand the meaning of mercy; and to strive to be sensitive to the frailty of Nature ...

> Translation from William Theodore de Bary, ed., *Sources of Japanese Tradition*
> (New York, 1958), pp. 786–91.

DOCUMENT 6   **DRAFT OF BASIC PLAN FOR THE ESTABLISHMENT OF THE GREATER EAST ASIA CO-PROSPERITY SPHERE, 1942**

This Plan was created in January 1942 by the Total War Research Institute, under the Army and the Cabinet. It maps out Japan's plans for the eventual domination of Asia.

Part I. Outline of Construction

The Plan. The Japanese empire is a manifestation of morality and its special characteristic is the propagation of the Imperial Way. It strives but for the achievement of *Hakko Ichiu* ['Eight corners under one roof', a phrase meaning Japan's dominion over Asia] , the spirit of its founding. ... It is necessary to foster the increased power of the empire, to cause East Asia to return to its original form of independence and co-prosperity by shaking off the yoke of Europe and America, and to let its countries and peoples develop their respective abilities in peaceful cooperation and secure livelihood.

The Form of East Asiatic Independence and Co-Prosperity. The states, their citizens, and resources, comprised in those areas pertaining to the Pacific, Central Asia, and the Indian Oceans formed into one general union are to be established as an autonomous zone of peaceful living and common prosperity on behalf of the peoples of the nations of East Asia. The area including Japan, Manchuria, North China, the lower Yangtze River, and the Russian Maritime Province, forms the nucleus of the East Asiatic Union. The Japanese empire possesses a duty as the leader of the East Asiatic Union.

The above purpose presupposes the inevitable emancipation or independence of Eastern Siberia, China, Indo-China, the South Seas, Australia, and India.

Regional Division in the East Asiatic Union and the National Defense Sphere for the Japanese Empire. In the Union of East Asia, the Japanese empire is at once the stabilizing power and the leading influence. To enable the empire actually to become the central influence in East Asia, the first necessity is the consolidation of the inner belt of East Asia; and the East Asiatic Sphere shall be divided as follows for this purpose:

The Inner Sphere – the vital sphere for the empire – includes Japan, Manchuria, North China, the lower Yangtze Area and the Russian Maritime area.

The Smaller Co-Prosperity Sphere – the smaller self-supplying sphere of East Asia – includes the inner sphere plus Eastern Siberia, China, Indo-China and the South Seas.

The Greater Co-Prosperity Sphere – the larger self-supplying sphere of East Asia – includes the smaller co-prosperity sphere, plus Australia, India, and island groups in the Pacific. ...

The Building of the National Strength. Since the Japanese empire is the center and pioneer of Oriental moral and cultural reconstruction, the officials and people of this country must return to the spirit of the Orient and acquire a thorough understanding of the spirit of the national moral character ...

Chapter 4. Thought and Cultural Construction

General Aim in Thought. The ultimate aim in thought construction in East Asia is to make East Asiatic peoples revere the imperial influence by propagating the Imperial Way based on the spirit of construction, and to establish the belief that uniting solely under this influence is the one and only way to the eternal growth and development of East Asia.

And during the next twenty years (the period during which the above ideal is to be reached) it is necessary to make the nations and peoples of East Asia realize the historical significance of the establishment of the New Order in East Asia, and in the common consciousness of East Asiatic unity, to liberate East Asia from the shackles of Europe and America and to establish the common conviction of constructing a New Order based on East Asiatic morality.

Occidental individualism and materialism shall be rejected and a moral world view, the basic principle of whose morality shall be the Imperial Way, shall be established. The ultimate object to be achieved is not exploitation but co-prosperity and mutual help, not competitive conflict but mutual assistance and mild peace, not a formal view of equality but a view of order based on righteous classification, not an idea of rights but an idea of service, and not several world views but one unified world view ...

From *Draft of Basic Plan*, International Military Tribunal for the Far East, International Prosecution Section, Document 2402B, Exhibit 1336. This translation from William Theodore de Bary, ed., *Sources of Japanese Tradition* (New York, 1958), pp. 801–5.

DOCUMENT 7   THE ESSENTIALS FOR CARRYING OUT THE EMPIRE'S POLICIES, 1941

This policy, in which the Japanese government resolved to begin the preparations for the bombing of Pearl Harbor and war with the United States, was adopted by the Imperial Conference on 6 September 1941.

In view of the current critical situation, in particular, the offensive attitudes that such countries as the United States, Great Britain, and the Netherlands are taking toward Japan, and in view of the situation in the Soviet Union and the condition of our Empire's national power, we will carry out our policy toward the South, which is contained in the 'Outline of National Policies in View of the Changing Situation' as follows:

I. Our Empire, for the purposes of self-defense and self-preservation, will complete preparations for war, with the last ten days of October as a tentative deadline, resolved to go to war with the United States, Great Britain, and the Netherlands if necessary.

II. Our Empire will concurrently take all possible diplomatic measures *vis-à-vis* the United States and Great Britain, and thereby endeavor to attain our objectives. The minimum objectives of our Empire to be attained through negotiations with the United States and Great Britain and the maximum concessions therein to be made by our Empire are noted in the attached documents.

III. In the event that there is no prospect of our demands being met by the first ten days of October through the diplomatic negotiations mentioned above, we will immediately decide to commence hostilities against the United States, Britain, and the Netherlands.

Policies other than those toward the South will be based on established national policy; and we will especially try to prevent the United States and the Soviet Union from forming a united front against Japan.

Statement by Prime Minister Konoe Fumimaro:
As you all know, the international situation in which we are involved has become increasingly strained; and in particular, the United States, Great Britain, and the Netherlands have come to oppose our Empire with all available means. There has also emerged the prospect that the United States and the Soviet Union will form a united front against Japan as the war between Germany and the Soviet Union becomes prolonged.

If we allow this situation to continue, it is inevitable that our Empire will gradually lose the ability to maintain its national power, and that our national power will lag behind that of the United States, Great Britain, and others. Under these circumstances our Empire must, of course, quickly prepare to meet any situation that may occur, and at the same time it must try to prevent the disaster of war by resorting to all possible diplomatic measures. If the diplomatic measures should fail to bring about favorable results within a certain period, I believe we cannot help but take the ultimate step in order to defend ourselves.

The Government and the Army and Navy sections of Imperial Headquarters have discussed this matter on numerous occasions. They have now reached an agreement, and have drafted 'The Essentials for Carrying Out the Empire's Policies,' which is on today's agenda. I would like you to consider this proposal carefully.

Items explained by Navy Chief of Staff Nagano Osami:
As the Prime Minister has explained in general terms, it is clear that our Empire must exert every effort to overcome the present difficult situation by peaceful means and must find a way to ensure her future prosperity and security. However, in the event that a peaceful solution is not attainable, and we have no alternative but to resort to war, the Supreme Command believes, from the standpoint of operations, that we cannot avoid being finally reduced to a crippled condition [if we delay for too long]. A number of vital military supplies, including oil, are dwindling day by day. This will cause a gradual weakening of our national defense, and lead to a situation in which, if we maintain the status quo, the capacity of our Empire to act will be reduced in the days to come. Meanwhile, the defenses of American, British, and other foreign military facilities and vital points in the Far East, and the military preparedness of these countries, particularly of the United States, are being strengthened with great speed. By the latter half of next year America's military preparedness will have made great progress, and it will be difficult to cope with her. Therefore, it must be said that it would be very dangerous for our Empire to remain idle and let the days go by ...

Our Empire does not have the means to take the offensive, overcome the enemy, and make them give up their will to fight. Moreover, we are short of resources at home, so we would very much like to avert a prolonged war. However, if we get into a prolonged war, the most important means of assuring that we will be able to bear this burden will be to seize the enemy's important military areas and sources of materials quickly at the beginning of the war, making our operational position tenable and at the same time obtaining vital materials from the areas now under hostile influence. If this first stage in our operations is carried out successfully, our Empire will have secured strategic areas in the Southwest Pacific, established an impregnable position, and laid the basis for a prolonged war, even if American military preparedness should proceed as scheduled. What happens thereafter will depend to a great extent on overall national power – including various elements, tangible and intangible – and on developments in the world situation ...

Items explained by Army Chief of Staff Sugiyama Gen:
... If we remain idle and mark time in these pressing circumstances, and if we let ourselves be trapped by the intrigues of Great Britain and the United States, our national defense capability will decline as time goes on; by contrast, the military preparedness of Great Britain, the United States, and other countries will be gradually strengthened. Then it will become more difficult to carry out military operations, and it is likely that we might eventually be unable to overcome the obstacles posed by Great Britain and the United States. Therefore, in order to begin hostilities while we are still confident that we can carry on a war with the United States and Great Britain, we have selected the last ten days of October as the time to complete our preparedness for war – taking into account meteorological and other conditions in the expected operational areas and the time needed for the mobilization of manpower, the requisitioning and equipping of ships, and the deployment of our military forces at important strategic points by long-distance sea transport ...

However, if there is no prospect that we will be able to achieve our aims through diplomatic measures by a certain time, it is necessary to decide promptly at that point to go to war with the United States and Great Britain, as well as to accelerate our war preparations. Thus we have to send reinforcements to southern French Indochina and complete other war preparations by the last ten days in October, the deadline. Therefore, I believe that when we take into account the movement of these forces, we must make the decision for war no later than the first ten days in October. With regard to the Northern Question while we are fighting in the South, I believe we need not worry. Ever since the outbreak of the German–Soviet war we have been strengthening our preparedness for a possible war with the Soviet Union, and we are ready for any unexpected development.

Statement by Director of the Planning Board Suzuki:
With regard to manpower and the morale of the people, which are the sources of our Empire's national power, I believe we can rest assured, whatever situation our Empire may face in the future.

The only problem concerns material resources. Our economy developed by being traditionally dependent on trade with Great Britain, the United States, and the British Empire. Accordingly, we depend on foreign sources to supply many of our vital materials ...

Our liquid fuel stockpile, which is the most important, will reach bottom by June or July of next year, even if we impose strict wartime control on the civilian demand.

President of the Privy Council Hara Yoshimichi
When I glance at Sections I, II, and III of the draft proposal, I notice that we

are to make war preparations and carry on diplomacy simultaneously, in the interests of defense and self-preservation. Also, a determination to commence hostilities seems to be implied. There are some passages suggesting that it may not be possible to avoid an outbreak of war, but that we will try to solve the matter by diplomatic means if this is at all possible. It thus appears that war comes first and diplomacy second. However, I take it that starting now, we will prepare for war at the same time that diplomatic measures are being used; that is, everywhere we will try to break the deadlock through diplomacy, but if this should fail, we will have to go to war. The draft seems to suggest that the war comes first, and diplomacy second; but I interpret it to mean that we will spare no efforts in diplomacy and we will go to war only when we can find no other way ...

Nobutaka, Ike, ed., *Japan's Decision for War: Records of the 1941 Policy Conferences* (Stanford, CA, 1967), pp. 135–49.

DOCUMENT 8   **THE POTSDAM DECLARATION, 1945**

The Potsdam Declaration outlined the Allied terms for ending the war with Japan: Japan's unconditional surrender.

July 26, 1945

(1)   WE – THE PRESIDENT of the United States, the President of the National Government of the Republic of China, and the Prime Minister of Great Britain, representing the hundreds of millions of our countrymen, have conferred and agree that Japan shall be given an opportunity to end this war.

(2)   The prodigious land, sea and air forces of the United States, of the British Empire and of China, many times reinforced by their armies and air fleets from the west, are poised to strike the final blows upon Japan. This military power is sustained and inspired by the determination of all the Allied Nations to prosecute the war against Japan until she ceases to resist.

(3)   The result of the futile and senseless German resistance to the might of the aroused free peoples of the world stands forth in awful clarity as an example to the people of Japan. The might that now converges on Japan is immeasurably greater than that which, when applied to the resisting Nazis, necessarily laid waste to the lands, the industry, and the method of life of the whole German people. The full application of our military power, backed by our resolve, will mean the inevitable and complete destruction of the Japanese armed forces and just as inevitably the utter devastation of the Japanese homeland.

(4)   The time has come for Japan to decide whether she will continue to

be controlled by those self-willed militaristic advisers whose unintelligent calculations have brought the Empire of Japan to the threshold of annihilation, or whether she will follow the path of reason.

(5)   Following are our terms. We will not deviate from them. There are no alternatives. We shall brook no delay.

(6)   There must be eliminated for all time the authority and influence of those who have deceived and misled the people of Japan into embarking on world conquest, for we insist that a new order of peace, security and justice will be impossible until irresponsible militarism is driven from the world.

(7)   Until such a new order is established and until there is convincing proof that Japan's war-making power is destroyed, points in Japanese territory to be designated by the Allies shall be occupied to secure the achievement of the basic objectives we are here setting forth.

(8)   The terms of the Cairo Declaration shall be carried out and Japanese sovereignty shall be limited to the islands of Honshu, Hokkaido, Kyushu, Shikoku and such minor islands as we determine.

(9)   The Japanese military forces, after being completely disarmed, shall be permitted to return to their homes with the opportunity to lead peaceful and productive lives.

(10)   We do not intend that the Japanese shall be enslaved as a race or destroyed as a nation, but stern justice shall be meted out to all war criminals, including those who have visited cruelties upon our prisoners. The Japanese Government shall remove all obstacles to the revival and strengthening of democratic tendencies among the Japanese people. Freedom of speech, of religion, and of thought, as well as respect for the fundamental human rights shall be established.

(11)   Japan shall be permitted to maintain such industries as will sustain her economy and permit the exaction of just reparations in kind, but not those which would enable her to re-arm for war. To this end, access to, as distinguished from control of, raw materials shall be permitted. Eventual Japanese participation in world trade relations shall be permitted.

(12)   The occupying forces of the Allies shall be withdrawn from Japan as soon as these objectives have been accomplished and there has been established in accordance with the freely expressed will of the Japanese people a peacefully inclined and responsible government.

(13)   We call upon the government of Japan to proclaim now the unconditional surrender of all Japanese armed forces, and to provide proper and adequate assurances of their good faith in such action. The alternative for Japan is prompt and utter destruction.

US Department of State, *Occupation of Japan: Policy and Progress*, Publication 2671, Far Eastern Series 17 (Washington, DC, 1946), pp. 53–5.

DOCUMENT 9   THE IMPERIAL RESCRIPT OF 14 AUGUST 1945

By this Rescript, broadcast over the radio on 15 August, Emperor Hirohito announced Japan's surrender to the Japanese people.

Our Good and Loyal Subjects:

After pondering deeply the general trends of the world and the actual conditions obtaining in Our Empire today, We have decided to effect a settlement of the present situation by resorting to an extraordinary measure.

We have ordered Our Government to communicate to the Governments of the United States, Great Britain, China and the Soviet Union that Our Empire accepts the provisions of their Joint Declaration.

To strive for the common prosperity and happiness of all nations as well as the security and well-being of Our subjects is the solemn obligation which has been handed down by Our Imperial Ancestors, and which We lay close to heart. Indeed, We declared war on America and Britain out of Our sincere desire to ensure Japan's self preservation and the stabilization of East Asia, it being far from Our thought either to infringe upon the sovereignty of other nations or to embark upon territorial aggrandizement. But now the war has lasted for nearly four years. Despite the best that has been done by everyone – the gallant fighting of military and naval forces, the diligence and assiduity of Our servants of the State and the devoted service of Our one hundred million people, the war situation has developed not necessarily to Japan's advantage, while the general trends of the world have all turned against her interest. Moreover, the enemy has begun to employ a new and most cruel bomb, the power of which to do damage is indeed incalculable, taking the toll of many innocent lives. Should We continue to fight, it would not only result in an ultimate collapse and obliteration of the Japanese nation, but also it would lead to the total extinction of human civilization. Such being the case, how are We to save the millions of Our subjects; or to atone Ourselves before the hallowed spirits of Our Imperial Ancestors? This is the reason why We have ordered the acceptance of the provisions of the Joint Declaration of the Powers.

We cannot but express the deepest sense of regret to our Allied nations of East Asia, who have consistently cooperated with the Empire towards the emancipation of East Asia. The thought of those officers and men as well as others who have fallen in the fields of battle, those who died at their posts of duty, or those who met with untimely death and all their bereaved families, pains Our heart night and day. The welfare of the wounded and the war-sufferers, and of those who have lost their homes and livelihood, are the objects of Our profound solicitude. The hardships and sufferings to which Our nation is to be subjected hereafter will be certainly great. We are keenly aware of the inmost feelings of all ye, Our subjects. However, it is according to the dictate of time and fate that We have resolved to pave the way for a grand peace for all the generations to come by enduring the unendurable and suffering what is insufferable.

Having been able to safeguard and maintain the structure of the Imperial State, We are always with ye, Our good and loyal subjects, relying upon your sincerity and integrity. Beware most strictly of any outbursts of emotion which may engender needless complications, or any fraternal contention and strife which may create confusion, lead ye astray and cause ye to lose the confidence of the world. Let the entire nation continue as one family from generation to generation, ever firm in its faith of the imperishableness of its divine land, and mindful of its heavy burden of responsibilities, and the long road before it. Unite your total strength to be devoted to the construction for the future. Cultivate the ways of rectitude; foster nobility of spirit; and work with resolution so as ye may enhance the innate glory of the Imperial State and keep pace with the progress of the world.

(Imperial Sign Manual)

(Imperial Seal)

The 14th day of the 8th month
of the 20th year of Showa.

From *The Oriental Economist*, Vol. XII (July–August 1945), p. 254. This translation from Robert J.C. Butow, *Japan's Decision to Surrender* (Stanford, CA, 1954), p. 248.

DOCUMENT 10   **THE INSTRUMENT OF SURRENDER, 1945**

This document, signed on the deck of the US battleship Missouri *in Tokyo Bay on 2 September 1945, formalized Japan's surrender of 15 August 1945.*

2 September 1945 (Tokyo Time)
We, acting by command of and in behalf of the Emperor of Japan, the Japanese Government and the Japanese Imperial General Headquarters, hereby accept the provisions set forth in the declaration issued by the heads of the Governments of the United States, China and Great Britain on 26 July 1945, at Potsdam, and subsequently adhered to by the Union of Soviet Socialist Republics, which four powers are hereafter referred to as the Allied Powers.

We hereby proclaim the unconditional surrender to the Allied Powers of the Japanese Imperial General Headquarters and of all Japanese armed forces and all armed forces under Japanese control wherever situated.

We hereby command all Japanese forces wherever situated and the Japanese people to cease hostilities forthwith, to preserve and save from damage all ships, aircraft, and military and civil property and to comply with all requirements which may be imposed by the Supreme Commander for the Allied Powers or by agencies of the Japanese Government at his direction.

We hereby command the Japanese Imperial General Headquarters to issue at once orders to the Commanders of all Japanese forces and all forces under Japanese control wherever situated to surrender unconditionally themselves and all forces under their control.

We hereby command all civil, military and naval officials to obey and enforce all proclamations, orders and directives deemed by the Supreme Commander for the Allied Powers to be proper to effectuate this surrender and issued by him or under his authority and we direct all such officials to remain at their posts and to continue to perform their non-combatant duties unless specifically relieved by him or under his authority.

We hereby undertake for the Emperor, the Japanese Government and their successors to carry out the provisions of the Potsdam Declaration in good faith, and to issue whatever orders and take whatever action may be required by the Supreme Commander for the Allied Powers or by any other designated representative of the Allied Powers for the purpose of giving effect to that Declaration.

We hereby command the Japanese Imperial Government and the Japanese Imperial General Headquarters at once to liberate all Allied prisoners of war and civilian internees now under Japanese control and to provide for their protection, care, maintenance and immediate transportation to places as directed.

The authority of the Emperor and the Japanese Government to rule the state shall be subject to the Supreme Commander for the Allied Powers who will take such steps as he deems proper to effectuate those terms of surrender.

Signed at *Tokyo Bay, Japan* at *0904 I* on the *second* day of *September*, 1945.

MAMORU SHIGEMITSU

By Command and in behalf of the Emperor of Japan and the Japanese Government.

YOSHIJIRO UMEZU

By Command and in behalf of the Japanese Imperial General Headquarters.

Accepted at *Tokyo Bay, Japan*, at *0908 I* on the *second* day of *September,* 1945, for the United States, Republic of China, United Kingdom and the Union of Soviet Socialist Republics, and in the interests of the other United Nations at war with Japan.

DOUGLAS MACARTHUR
Supreme Commander for the Allied Powers.

US Department of State, *Occupation of Japan: Policy and Progress,* Publication 2671, Far Eastern Series 17 (Washington, DC, 1946), pp. 62–3.

DOCUMENT 11   THE BASIC INITIAL POST-SURRENDER DIRECTIVE, 1945

This document outlined in broad strokes the basic military, political, economic and social objectives of the US in the Allied Occupation of Japan.

Part I – Ultimate Objectives

August 29, 1945
The ultimate objectives of the United States in regard to Japan, to which policies in the initial period must conform, are:

(a) To insure that Japan will not again become a menace to the United States or to the peace and security of the world.
(b) To bring about the eventual establishment of a peaceful and responsible government which will respect the rights of other states and will support the objectives of the United States as reflected in the ideals and principles of the Charter of the United Nations. The United States desires that this government should conform as closely as may be to principles of democratic self-government but it is not the responsibility of the Allied Powers to impose upon Japan any form of government not supported by the freely expressed will of the people.

These objectives will be achieved by the following principal means:

(a) Japan's sovereignty will be limited to the islands of Honshu, Hokkaido, Kyushu, Shikoku, and such minor outlying islands as may be determined, in accordance with the Cairo Declaration and other agreements to which the United States is or may be a party.
(b) Japan will be completely disarmed and demilitarized. The authority of the militarists and the influence of militarism will be totally eliminated from her political, economic and social life. Institutions expressive of the spirit of militarism and aggression will be vigorously suppressed.
(c) The Japanese people shall be encouraged to develop a desire for individual liberties and respect for fundamental human rights, particularly the freedoms of religion, assembly, speech, and the press. They shall also be encouraged to form democratic and representative organizations.

(d) The Japanese people shall be afforded opportunity to develop for themselves an economy which will permit the peacetime requirements of the population to be met.

Part II – Allied Authority

1. Military Occupation

There will be a military occupation of the Japanese home islands to carry into effect the surrender terms and further the achievement of the ultimate objectives stated above. The occupation shall have the character of an operation in behalf of the principal Allied powers acting in the interests of the United Nations at war with Japan. For that reason, participation of the forces of other nations that have taken a leading part in the war against Japan will be welcomed and expected. The occupation forces will be under the command of a Supreme Commander designated by the United States.

Although every effort will be made, by consultation and by constitution of appropriate advisory bodies, to establish policies for the conduct of the occupation and the control of Japan which will satisfy the principal Allied powers, in the event of any differences of opinion among them, the policies of the United States will govern.

2. Relationship to Japanese Government

The authority of the emperor and the Japanese government will be subject to the Supreme Commander, who will possess all powers necessary to effectuate the surrender terms and to carry out the policies established for the conduct of the occupation and the control of Japan.

In view of the present character of Japanese society and the desire of the United States to attain its objectives with a minimum commitment of its forces and resources, the Supreme Commander will exercise his authority through Japanese governmental machinery and agencies, including the emperor, to the extent that this satisfactorily furthers United States objectives. The Japanese government will be permitted, under his instructions, to exercise the normal powers of government in matters of domestic administration. This policy, however, will be subject to the right and duty of the Supreme Commander to require changes in governmental machinery or personnel or to act directly if the emperor or other Japanese authority does not satisfactorily meet the requirements of the Supreme Commander in effectuating the surrender terms. This policy, moreover, does not commit the Supreme Commander to support the emperor or any other Japanese governmental authority in opposition to evolutionary changes looking toward the attainment of United States objectives. The policy is to use the existing form of government in Japan, not to support it. Changes in the form of government initiated by the Japanese people or government in the direction of modifying its feudal and authoritarian tendencies are to be permitted and favored. In the event that the effectuation of such changes involves the use of force by the Japanese people or government against persons opposed thereto, the Supreme Commander should intervene only where necessary to ensure the security of his forces and the attainment of all other objectives of the occupation.

3. Publicity as to Policies

The Japanese people, and the world at large, shall be kept fully informed of the objectives and policies of the occupation, and of progress made in their fulfillment.

Part III – Political

1. Disarmament and Demilitarization

Disarmament and demilitarization are the primary tasks of the military occupation and shall be carried out promptly and with determination. Every effort shall be made to bring home to the Japanese people the part played by the military and naval leaders, and those who collaborated with them, in bringing about the existing and future distress of the people.

Japan is not to have an army, navy, air force, secret police organization, or any civil aviation. Japan's ground, air, and naval forces shall be disarmed and disbanded and the Japanese Imperial General Headquarters, the General Staff, and all secret police organizations shall be dissolved. Military and naval matériel, military and naval vessels and military and naval installations, and military, naval, and civilian aircraft shall be surrendered and shall be disposed of as required by the Supreme Commander.

High officials of the Japanese Imperial General Headquarters, and General Staff, other high military and naval officials of the Japanese government, leaders of ultranationalist and militarist organizations, and other important exponents of militarism and aggression will be taken into custody and held for future disposition. Persons who have been active exponents of militarism and militant nationalism will be removed and excluded from public office and from any other position of public or substantial private responsibility. Ultranationalistic or militaristic social, political, professional, and commercial societies and institutions will be dissolved and prohibited.

Militarism and ultranationalism, in doctrine and practice, including paramilitary training, shall be eliminated from the educational system. Former career military and naval officers, both commissioned and noncommissioned, and all other exponents of militarism and ultranationalism shall be excluded from supervisory and teaching positions.

2. War Criminals

Persons charged by the Supreme Commander or appropriate United Nations agencies with being war criminals, including those charged with having visited cruelties upon United Nations prisoners or other nationals, shall be arrested, tried, and, if convicted, punished. Those wanted by another of the United Nations for offenses against its nationals, shall, if not wanted for trial or as witnesses or otherwise by the Supreme Commander, be turned over to the custody of such other nation.

3. Encouragement of Desire for Individual Liberties and Democratic
   Processes

Freedom of religious worship shall be proclaimed promptly on occupation. At the same time it should be made plain to the Japanese that ultra-nationalistic and militaristic organizations and movements will not be permitted to hide behind the cloak of religion.

The Japanese people shall be afforded opportunity and encouraged to become familiar with the history, institutions, culture, and the accomplishments of the United States and the other democracies. Association of personnel of the occupation forces with the Japanese population should be controlled only to the extent necessary to further the policies and objectives of the occupation.

Democratic political parties, with rights of assembly and public discussion, shall be encouraged, subject to the necessity for maintaining the security of the occupying forces.

Laws, decrees and regulations which establish discrimination on grounds of race, nationality, creed, or political opinion shall be abrogated; those which conflict with the objectives and policies outlined in this document shall be repealed, suspended, or amended as required; and agencies charged specifically with their enforcement shall be abolished or appropriately modified. Persons unjustly confined by Japanese authority on political grounds shall be released. The judicial, legal, and police systems shall be reformed as soon as practicable to conform to the policies set forth in Articles 1 and 3 of this Part III and thereafter shall be progressively influenced, to protect individual liberties and civil rights.

Part IV – Economic

1. Economic Demilitarization

The existing economic basis of Japanese military strength must be destroyed and not be permitted to revive.

Therefore, a program will be enforced containing the following elements, among others: the immediate cessation and future prohibition of production of all goods designed for the equipment, maintenance, or use of any military force or establishment; the imposition of a ban upon any specialized facilities for the production or repair of implements of war, including naval vessels and all forms of aircraft; the institution of a system of inspection and control over selected elements in Japanese economic activity to prevent concealed or disguised military preparation; the elimination in Japan of those selected industries or branches of production whose chief value to Japan is in preparing for war; the prohibition of specialized research and instruction directed to the development of war-making power; and the limitation of the size and character of Japan's heavy industries to its future peaceful requirements, and restriction of Japanese merchant shipping to the extent required to accomplish the objectives of demilitarization.

The eventual disposition of those existing production facilities within Japan which are to be eliminated in accord with this program, as between conversion to other uses, transfer abroad, and scrapping will be determined after inventory. Pending decision, facilities readily convertible for civilian production should not be destroyed, except in emergency situations.

2. Promotion of Democratic Forces

Encouragement shall be given and favor shown to the development of organizations, in labor, industry, and agriculture, organized on a democratic basis. Policies shall be favored which permit a wide distribution of income and of the ownership of the means of production and trade.

Those forms of economic activity, organization, and leadership shall be favored that are deemed likely to strengthen the peaceful disposition of the Japanese people, and to make it difficult to command or direct economic activity in support of military ends.

To this end it shall be the policy of the Supreme Commander:

(a)   To prohibit the retention in or selection for places of importance in the economic field of individuals who do not direct future Japanese economic effort solely towards peaceful ends; and

(b)   To favor a program for the dissolution of the large industrial and banking combinations which have exercised control of a great part of Japan's trade and industry.

US Department of State, *Occupation of Japan: Policy and Progress*, Publication 2671, Far Eastern Series 17 (Washington, DC, 1946), pp. 73–81.

DOCUMENT 12   **THE CONSTITUTION OF JAPAN, 1947**

After a Japanese committee returned a constitutional draft to Occupation authorities that was little changed from the Meiji Constitution, MacArthur instructed an Occupation group to write a new Constitution, giving them six days to complete the job.

We, the Japanese people, acting through our duly elected representatives in the National Diet, determined that we shall secure for ourselves and our posterity the fruits of peaceful cooperation with all nations and the blessings of liberty throughout this land, and resolved that never again shall we be visited with the horrors of war through the action of government, do proclaim that sovereign power resides with the people and do firmly establish this Constitution. Government is a sacred trust of the people, the authority for which is derived from the people, the powers of which are exercised by the representatives of the people, and the benefits of which are enjoyed by the people. This is a universal principle of mankind upon which this Constitution is founded. We reject and revoke all constitutions, laws, ordinances, and rescripts in conflict herewith.

We, the Japanese people, desire peace for all time and are deeply conscious of the high ideals controlling human relationship, and we have determined to preserve our security and existence, trusting in the justice and faith of the peace-loving peoples of the world. We desire to occupy an honored place in an international society striving for the preservation of peace, and the banishment of tyranny and slavery, oppression and intolerance for all time from the earth. We recognize that all peoples of the world have the right to live in peace, free from fear and want.

We believe that no nation is responsible to itself alone, but that laws of political morality are universal; and that obedience to such laws is incumbent upon all nations who would sustain their own sovereignty and justify their sovereign relationship with other nations.

We, the Japanese people, pledge our national honor to accomplish these high ideals and purposes with all our resources.

CHAPTER I. The Emperor
ARTICLE 1. The Emperor shall be the symbol of the State and of the unity of the people, deriving his position from the will of the people with whom resides sovereign power.

ARTICLE 2. The Imperial Throne shall be dynastic and succeeded to in accordance with the Imperial House Law passed by the Diet.

ARTICLE 3. The advice and approval of the Cabinet shall be required for all acts of the Emperor in matters of state, and the Cabinet shall be responsible therefor.

ARTICLE 4. The Emperor shall perform only such acts in matters of state as are provided for in this Constitution and he shall not have powers related to government.

2. The Emperor may delegate the performance of his acts in matters of state as may be provided by law.

ARTICLE 5. When, in accordance with the Imperial House Law, a Regency is established, the Regent shall perform his acts in matters of state in the Emperor's name. In this case, paragraph one of the preceding article will be applicable.

ARTICLE 6. The Emperor shall appoint the Prime Minister as designated by the Diet.

2. The Emperor shall appoint the Chief Judge of the Supreme Court as designated by the Cabinet.

ARTICLE 7. The Emperor, with the advice and approval of the Cabinet, shall perform the following acts in matters of state on behalf of the people:

(1) Promulgation of amendments of the constitution, laws, cabinet orders and treaties;

(2) Convocation of the Diet;

(3) Dissolution of the House of Representatives;

(4) Proclamation of general election of members of the Diet;

(5) Attestation of the appointment and dismissal of Ministers of State and other officials as provided for by law, and of full powers and credentials of Ambassadors and Ministers;

(6) Attestation of general and special amnesty, commutation of punishment, reprieve, and restoration of rights;

(7) Awarding of honors;

(8) Attestation of instruments of ratification and other diplomatic documents as provided for by law;

(9) Receiving foreign ambassadors and ministers;

(10) Performance of ceremonial functions.

ARTICLE 8. No property can be given to, or received by, the Imperial House, nor can any gifts be made therefrom, without the authorization of the Diet.

CHAPTER II. Renunciation of War
ARTICLE 9. Aspiring sincerely to an international peace based on justice and order, the Japanese people forever renounce war as a sovereign right of the nation and the threat or use of force as means of settling international disputes.

2. In order to accomplish the aim of the preceding paragraph, land, sea, and air forces, as well as other war potential, will never be maintained. The right of belligerency of the state will not be recognized.

CHAPTER III. Rights and Duties of the People
ARTICLE 13. All of the people shall be respected as individuals. Their right to life, liberty, and the pursuit of happiness shall, to the extent that it does not interfere with the public welfare, be the supreme consideration in legislation and in other governmental affairs.

ARTICLE 14. All of the people are equal under the law and there shall be no discrimination in political, economic or social relations because of race, creed, sex, social status or family origin.

2. Peers and peerage shall not be recognized.

3. No privilege shall accompany any award of honor, decoration or any distinction, nor shall any such award be valid beyond the lifetime of the individual who now holds or hereafter may receive it.

ARTICLE 15. The people have the inalienable right to choose their public officials and to dismiss them.

2. All public officials are servants of the whole community and not of any group thereof.

3. Universal adult suffrage is guaranteed with regard to the election of public officials.

4. In all elections, secrecy of the ballot shall not be violated. A voter shall not be answerable, publicly or privately, for the choice he has made.

ARTICLE 19. Freedom of thought and conscience shall not be violated.

ARTICLE 20. Freedom of religion is guaranteed to all. No religious organization shall receive any privileges from the State nor exercise any political authority.

2. No person shall be compelled to take part in any religious act, celebration, rite or practice.

3. The State and its organs shall refrain from religious education or any other religious activity.

ARTICLE 21. Freedom of assembly and association as well as speech, press and all other forms of expression are guaranteed.

2. No censorship shall be maintained, nor shall the secrecy of any means of communication be violated.

ARTICLE 23. Academic freedom is guaranteed.

ARTICLE 24. Marriage shall be based only on the mutual consent of both sexes and it shall be maintained through mutual cooperation with the equal rights of husband and wife as a basis.

2. With regard to choice of spouse, property rights, inheritance, choice of domicile, divorce and other matters pertaining to marriage and the family, laws shall be enacted from the standpoint of individual dignity and the essential equality of the sexes.

ARTICLE 25. All people shall have the right to maintain the minimum standards of wholesome and cultured living.

2. In all spheres of life, the State shall use its endeavors for the promotion and extension of social welfare and security, and of public health.

ARTICLE 26. All people shall have the right to receive an equal education correspondent to their ability, as provided by law.

2. All people shall be obligated to have all boys and girls under their protection receive ordinary education as provided for by law. Such compulsory education shall be free.

ARTICLE 27. All people shall have the right and the obligation to work.

2. Standards for wages, hours, rest and other working conditions shall be fixed by law.

3. Children shall not be exploited.

ARTICLE 28. The right of workers to organize and to bargain and act collectively is guaranteed.

ARTICLE 34. No person shall be arrested or detained without being at once informed of the charges against him or without the immediate privilege of counsel; nor shall he be detained without adequate cause; and upon demand of any person such cause must be immediately shown in open court in his presence and the presence of his counsel.

CHAPTER IV. The Diet

ARTICLE 41. The Diet shall be the highest organ of state power, and shall be the sole law-making organ of the State.

ARTICLE 42. The Diet shall consist of two Houses, namely the House of Representatives and the House of Councillors.

ARTICLE 43. Both Houses shall consist of elected members, representative of all the people.

US Department of State, *Occupation of Japan: Policy and Progress*, Publication 2671, Far Eastern Series 17 (Washington, DC, 1946), pp. 117–32. Also reprinted in Daikichi Irokawa, *The Age of Hirohito: In Search of Modern Japan* (New York, 1995), pp. 148–52.

GLOSSARY

Anti-Comintern Pact Concluded by Prime Minister Hirota Koki in November 1936. Japan and Germany agreed to a mutual exchange of information about the Comintern and to work together to limit its effect. A secret protocol stipulated that if either nation was attacked by the Soviets, the other would refrain from any activities that would help the Soviets.

Article 9 (Peace Clause) In the postwar 1947 Japanese Constitution, Article 9 declares that 'the Japanese people forever renounce war as a sovereign right ... land, sea and air forces, as well as other war potential, will never be maintained.' This 'Peace Clause' was promoted by General MacArthur. When the Korean War broke out in 1950 the Article was interpreted to allow for self-defense capabilities, and Japan today maintains a large Self-Defense Force.

China Incident While Japanese troops were conducting maneuvers just outside Beijing in July 1937, a clash broke out with nearby Chinese troops. Though Prime Minister Konoe sought a local settlement, Chinese leader Chiang Kaishek was pressured to take a more aggressive stance. When war broke out on 7 July 1937, the Japanese leadership believed it would be a short war, but fighting continued until 15 August 1945.

Exclusion Act In 1924 the US Congress passed an act limiting Japanese immigration to the United States, setting off a wave of anti-American demonstrations in Japan and contributing to a broad feeling of resentment toward the West.

15 May Incident As part of the Showa Restoration attempts of the early 1930s, the 15 May Incident was planned and carried out in 1932 by young members of the ultra-nationalist group Ketsumeidan in concert with Navy officers and Army cadets. Seeking to effect a restoration of direct imperial rule, the group unleashed a burst of violence against civilian governmental leaders. In the aftermath, Prime Minister Saito Makoto sought political harmony by creating a so-called 'cabinet of national unity.' (See 26 February Incident and Showa Restoration.)

Imperial Rule Assistance Association Prime Minister Konoe founded the IRAA in 1940 after the political parties voluntarily disbanded themselves. Konoe's aim was to quiet the political squabbling between the military, civilian bureaucracy, political parties and industrial interests. The IRAA was a single, unified political party that functioned primarily as a means of exercising control over the wartime population.

Independence of the Supreme Command The Meiji Constitution of 1890 stipulated that the military would be under the direct control of the Emperor, independent of civilian governmental control. Though not initially a problem, since during the Meiji period the oligarchs who drafted the Constitution also advised the Emperor and controlled the government, by the 1920s and 1930s problems arose as the military began to act increasingly independently, as for example in the Manchurian Incident of 1931.

Kanto Earthquake In 1923 a huge earthquake shook the Kanto Plain, on which Tokyo is located, killing over 100,000 people and injuring another 500,000. In the chaotic aftermath, riots broke out in which Koreans and other minorities, including radical intellectuals, were targeted by both the people and the police. The rebuilding effort proved to be a costly drain for Japan, then experiencing an economic downturn.

Kodoha (Imperial Way faction) Influential faction within the Army, with many younger supporters, the Kodoha believed Japan must prepare for war with the Soviet Union. They advocated direct, violent action to effect a 'Showa Restoration.' The Kodoha carried out the 26 February Incident in 1936. The purge of the faction in the aftermath of this incident left the opposing Toseiha in a dominant position in the Army.

Kwantung Army A division of the Japanese Imperial Army sent to guard Japanese leaseholds on the South Manchurian Railway and the Liaodong Peninsula in Kwantung province in China in 1907. The Kwantung Army attracted top soldiers. Advocating an aggressive Japanese stance toward China, the Kwantung Army took a leading role in pressing Japan's advantages in northern China and Manchuria.

Lytton Report In 1933 the League of Nations released the Lytton Report criticizing Japan's aggression in Manchuria and calling on Japan to withdraw from the region. Japan's response was to withdraw from the League of Nations, furthering its international isolation.

London Conference The London Conference of 1930 was designed to update the 1922 Washington Conference agreements on naval arms limitations. Japan hoped to increase its ratio of naval tonnage *vis-à-vis* Great Britain and the United States, but was unable to do so. Prime Minister Hamaguchi signed the London Conference treaty despite Navy objections, incurring the wrath of the Navy General Staff for having breached the 'Independence of the Supreme Command.'

Manchurian Incident (18 September 1931) Field grade officers of the Kwantung Army, hoping to expand hostilities in Manchuria and press Japan's advantage there, exploded a bomb on the South Manchurian Railroad just outside Mukden. Without authorization from the government in Tokyo, military reinforcements were sent to the area from Japan's colony in Korea. In February 1932, Manchuria was made into the Japanese puppet state Manchukuo. The incident and its aftermath led to increased international isolation for Japan, and resulted in the military taking control of foreign affairs until the end of the Pacific War in 1945.

Midway, Battle of Fought near the Island of Midway in early June 1942. The brainchild of Admiral Yamamoto Isoroku, who threatened to resign if not allowed to pursue the plan for a surprise attack designed to eliminate the remnants of the US Pacific fleet that escaped destruction at Pearl Harbor. US intelligence broke the Japanese code, and, forewarned of the attack, the US prevailed despite their underdog status. Four Japanese carriers were destroyed in the battle, and the battle, Japan's last offensive action, became a turning point in the Pacific War.

New Order in East Asia In November 1938, Prime Minister Konoe announced Japan's goals to build a 'New Order in East Asia,' harping on such themes as 'Asia for the Asians,' and a self-sufficient Asia free from Western interference. This idea became a cornerstone of Japan's efforts to subdue Asia during the Pacific War.

1947 Constitution Postwar Constitution, ratifed by the Diet and effective from May 1947, placed sovereignty in the people and made the emperor a 'symbol of the state and of the unity of the people.' Granted Japanese citizens basic human rights including equal rights for men and women; made the Diet the highest organ of the state; eliminated Japan's right to maintain war potential. (See Reverse Course, Article 9.)

Peace Preservation Law (1925) Passed in March 1925, directly following the enactment of the Universal Manhood Suffrage Law. Designed to reign in excessive political activity, the Peace Preservation Law outlawed any organization that advocated an end to the system of private property and any group that advocated a change in the emperor system. Amended in 1928 to allow for the death penalty, the law was again expanded in 1941 to provide for 'preventative arrest' and was an important tool in the government's exercise of control over the population up until its repeal in October 1945. (See Universal Manhood Suffrage Bill.)

Pearl Harbor Having failed to secure diplomatic access to Southeast Asian oil and faced with US demands for a return to the *status quo ante* 1931, Japan attacked the US Pacific Fleet at Pearl Harbor on 8 December 1941, hoping to bring the United States back to the negotiating table with a more favorable offer. Instead, the attack roused the United States from its isolation and resulted in an American declaration of war against both Japan and Germany.

Potsdam Declaration Meeting at Potsdam at the end of July 1945, the US, Britain and China agreed on the Potsdam Declaration, calling for Japan's unconditional surrender to end the Pacific War and outlining military, political and other reforms that Japan must subsequently adopt. The Soviet Union later agreed to the terms, which promised 'utter destruction' for Japan should it continue to fight. Despite serious concerns over the fate of the Emperor and the imperial institution, on 14 August 1945 Japan agreed to the unconditional surrender and shortly thereafter the Allied Occupation of Japan commenced.

Reverse Course In the late 1940s, as communism was taking root in mainland China and in North Korea and northern Viet Nam, Occupation policy began to shift away from the original goal of rebuilding Japan into a stable, pacifistic agrarian nation and began to focus on a Japan that would serve as the United States' bulwark against Asian communism. Early Occupation labor and economic reforms were modified and Article 9 of the 1947 Constitution was reinterpreted to allow Japan to maintain defensive military capability. (See 1947 Constitution and Article 9.)

San Francisco Peace Treaty The formal end to the Pacific War and the end of the Allied Occupation of Japan was arranged with the signing of the San Francisco Peace Treaty on 8 September 1951. The Treaty went into effect in April 1952. In it, Japan renounced claim to all territories acquired through aggression.

Showa Restoration The Showa Restoration encompassed a series of attempts in the early 1930s to remove civilian influence from government and to restore direct imperial rule, including the 15 May Incident of 1932 and the 26 February Incident of 1936. The conspirators in these efforts were generally younger members of the military, imbued with the emperor-centered ultra-nationalism that characterized Japanese society in the 1930s and early 1940s.

Tonarigumi Neighborhood groups of 10–20 households, the *tonarigumi* were organized by the IRAA in 1940 to promote the war effort and to provide for mutual surveillance. They functioned as the smallest administrative unit of the government and enabled the government to exercise minute control over the population.

Toseiha (Tosei faction) 'Control' faction in the Army, led by Tojo Hideki and Ishiwara Kanji, the Toseiha advocated economic and technological mobilization for war against China. Opposed by the Kodoha, the influence of the Toseiha increased after the 26 February Incident led to a purge of the Kodoha.

Tripartite Pact Japan signed the Tripartite Pact with Germany and Italy in Berlin on 27 September 1940. The signatories pledged that 'when and if any of the signatories were attacked by any third power not then engaged in the European War or the China Incident, (excluding the Soviet Union) the other two would aid her with all political, economic or military means' (see p. 62). Though the Pact did not lead to increased cooperation between Germany, Italy and Japan, it did result in a US embargo on the sale of scrap iron and steel to Japan.

Twenty-One Demands Series of demands Japan issued to China in 1915 designed to consolidate Japan's World War I gains there, the Twenty-One Demands included economic, military and political concessions. The Demands inspired widespread anti-Japanese feelings in China which contributed to Japan's growing insecurity *vis-à-vis* China.

26 February Incident (1936) Army coup attempt aimed at removing civilian officials around the throne and restoring direct imperial rule. For three days, 1,400 Army troops controlled downtown Tokyo until Emperor Hirohito indicated he did not support the coup. Led by the Kodo faction of the Army, the resulting purge strengthened Tosei faction influence in the Army. (See also 15 May Incident and Showa Restoration.)

United States–Japan Mutual Security Treaty The United States–Japan Mutual Security Treaty was signed in conjunction with the San Francisco Peace Treaty. Because the postwar Constitution prohibited Japan from maintaining anything but a defensive military capability, this Security Treaty provided Japan with US military protection, in exchange for which the US was granted the right to maintain military bases in Japan. Despite considerable opposition in Japan over the years, the treaty has been renewed between the two countries since it went into effect in 1952. The treaty has kept Japanese military expenditures relatively low, allowing Japan to concentrate its capital on industrial development. (See San Francisco Peace Treaty.)

Universal Manhood Suffrage Bill (1925) The Universal Manhood Suffrage Bill granted the vote to all non-indigent males over the age of 25, expanding the electorate from 3 million to 12.5 million. To calm conservative fears of political chaos, immediately prior to passing this bill the Diet passed the Peace Preservation Law. (See Peace Preservation Law.)

Zaibatsu Huge financial combines consisting of vertical monopolies. Because Occupation authorities believed they played a large role in promoting prewar and wartime militarism, and in an effort to introduce economic democratization to Japan, the *zaibatsu* were targeted for dissolution by the Occupation. The effort to eliminate the *zaibatsu*, however, is widely regarded as the least successful of the Occupation reforms, and similar financial organizations exist in Japan today, known as the *keiretsu*.

WHO'S WHO

Chiang Kaishek (1887–1975) Leader of the Chinese Nationalist Party, Chiang opposed fighting against the Japanese in the 1920s and 1930s, wanting to save his strength to exterminate the Chinese Communists. He was finally forced to enter into a United Front with the Communists in 1936. War with Japan broke out shortly thereafter.

Fukuzawa Yukichi (1835–1901) Leading proponent of democracy in the early Meiji period. Educator and popularizer of information about the West. Founder of Keio University and the newspaper *Jiji Shimpo*. Near the end of his life supported Japan's aggressive policies toward Asia.

Ishiwara Kanji (1889–1949) Lieutenant-Colonel in the Kwantung Army at the time of the Manchurian incident, Ishiwara played a major role in carrying out the incident, which led to the expansion of Japanese control over Manchuria in the early 1930s.

Kita Ikki (1884–1937) Leading philosopher of the ultra-nationalist movement. In his most influential book he stressed the organic unity of the people and the Emperor, and called for a violent coup to restore direct imperial rule. His ideas played a leading role in the 1936 26 February Incident, and he was executed in 1937 for allegedly having contributed to the plot.

Konoe Fumimaro (1891–1945) Prince Konoe served as Prime Minister with three different cabinets between June 1937 and October 1941. Sophisticated, urbane and indecisive, Konoe led Japan into war with China in 1937. He resigned the premiership in October 1941 rather than lead Japan into war with the United States, and committed suicide in December 1945 just prior to being arrested as a Class 'A' war criminal.

MacArthur, General Douglas (1880–1964) During the Pacific War MacArthur served as Commander-in-Chief of US forces in the Far East. After the war, as Supreme Commander for the Allied Powers (SCAP) MacArthur was in charge of the Allied Occupation of Japan and wielded immense power in that position. He was dismissed from the post by President Truman in 1951 due to disagreements over how to prosecute the war in Korea.

Matsuoka Yosuke (1880–1946) A career diplomat, Matsuoka supported an aggressive policy toward China. Served as Japan's delegate to the League of Nations and led Japan's walk-out over the Lytton Commission Report in 1933. Later pursued and concluded the Tripartite Pact, linking Japan to Germany and Italy. Volatile and unpredictable, Matsuoka alienated his colleagues. Arrested as a Class 'A' war criminal, Matsuoka died during the trial proceedings.

Minobe Tatsukichi (1873–1948) Professor of Law at Tokyo Imperial University, and prominent legal scholar. A leading proponent of the emperor organ theory, which held that the emperor was an organ of the state, Minobe was denounced for treason and forced to resign his post in the House of Peers. In 1936 he was the target of an assassination attempt. The popular reaction to his legal theories on the emperor served as a measure of the rising tide of ultra-nationalism.

Nomura Kichisaburo (1877–1964) A retired admiral, Nomura began his service as Japanese Ambassador to the United States from July 1940. As Ambassador, Nomura led negotiations between Japan and the US on the eve of the Pacific War.

Shidehara Kijuro (1872–1951) As Foreign Minister, 1924–27 and 1929–31, advocated the unpopular policy of non-intervention and non-expansion into China, instead favoring economic and trade ties. Served as Prime Minister in the postwar period, October 1945–May 1946.

Suzuki Kantaro (1868–1948) Respected senior statesman and retired admiral, Suzuki became Prime Minister in April 1945. Viewed by some as a possible 'peace advocate,' Suzuki approached the Soviet Union as a possible mediator to end the war, unaware that Stalin had agreed to join the war against Japan. Suzuki accepted the Potsdam Declaration on 14 August 1945 and resigned his office the following day.

Tanaka Giichi (1863–1929) Prime Minister, 1927–29, and architect of Japan's 'positive policy' toward China, outlining a more aggressive stance toward securing Japanese interests on the continent. Oversaw the amendment of the Peace Preservation Law to include the death sentence.

Tojo Hideki (1884–1948) Tokyo native and graduate of the Military Academy, Tojo rose through the ranks of the Kwantung Army and strongly supported Japan's aggressive policy toward China. A member of the Tosei faction in the Army, Tojo advocated war with China and believed war with the United States was inevitable. Served as War Minister in the Konoe Cabinet in 1940 and succeeded Konoe as Prime Minister in October 1941. He was forced out of office in July 1944 as the war situation worsened. Arrested as a Class 'A' war criminal, Tojo was executed by hanging in December 1948.

Yamamoto Isoroku (1884–1943) Admiral and chief architect of Japan's attack on Pearl Harbor and Midway, Yamamoto was a highly respected and hugely popular military leader and strategist. He was killed in 1943 when a special US mission shot down his plane over the Solomon Islands. His death left a big hole in Japan's strategic planning and morale.

Yoshida Shigeru (1878–1967) Conservative postwar Prime Minister during most of the 1946–54 period, Yoshida began his career in the Foreign Ministry and served as Japan's Ambassador to Italy and then to Britain in 1936–38. During the war years Yoshida largely avoided the political arena. He was arrested in early 1945 because of his close association with Britain and the United States. After Japan's surrender, however, he was elected Prime Minister. As Prime Minister, Yoshida promoted close military ties with the United States as a way to free up capital for industrial development.

Zhang Xueliang (Chang Hsueh-liang) (1901–) The 'Young Marshal,' son of Manchurian warlord Zhang Zuolin (Chang Tso-lin), Zhang Xueliang joined Chiang Kaishek's Nationalist forces after his father was assassinated by staff officers of Japan's Kwantung Army in 1928. In 1936 Zhang Xueliang participated in the kidnapping of Chiang Kaishek to force him to conclude a united front agreement with the Chinese Communist Party against the Japanese.

BIBLIOGRAPHY

WORKS CITED

Butow, Robert J.C., *Japan's Decision to Surrender* (Stanford, CA, 1954).

Butow, Robert J.C., *Tojo and the Coming of the War* (Stanford, CA, 1961).

Byas, Hugh, *Government by Assassination* (New York, 1942).

Chang, Iris, *The Rape of Nanjing: The Forgotten Holocaust of World War II* (New York, 1997).

Cook, Haruko Taya and Theodore F. Cook, eds, *Japan at War: An Oral History* (New York, 1992).

Coox, Alvin D., 'The Kwantung Army,' in Peter Duus, Ramon H. Myers and Mark R. Peattie, eds, *The Japanese Informal Empire in China, 1895–1937* (Princeton, NJ, 1989).

Crowley, James B., *Japan's Quest for Autonomy: National Security and Foreign Policy, 1930–1938* (Princeton, NJ, 1966).

Crowley, James B., 'A New Deal for East Asia: One Road to Pearl Harbor,' in James B. Crowley, ed., *Modern East Asia: Essays in Interpretation* (New York, 1970).

de Bary, William Theodore, ed., *Sources of Japanese Tradition* (New York, 1958).

Dore, R.P., 'Execution of Land Reform,' in *The Japan Reader 2* (New York, 1973).

Dower, John W., *Embracing Defeat: Japan in the Wake of World War II* (New York, 1999a).

Dower, John, *MacArthur*, documentary videotape produced for the Public Broadcasting System (1999b).

Duus, Peter, *The Rise of Modern Japan* (Boston, 1976).

Duus, Peter, *Modern Japan* (Boston, 1998).

Feis, Herbert, *The Road to Pearl Harbor: The Coming of the War Between the United States and Japan* (Princeton, NJ, 1950).

Ferrell, Robert H., review of *Weapons for Victory: The Hiroshima Decision Fifty Years Later*, by Robert James Maddox (New York, 1995) in *Continuity* 22 (Spring, 1998).

Frank, Richard B., *Downfall: The End of the Imperial Japanese Empire* (New York, 1999).

Fukuzawa, Yukichi, *The Autobiography of Fukuzawa Yukichi*, trans. Eiichi Kiyooka (Tokyo, 1948).

Fukuzawa, Yukichi, *An Outline Theory of Civilization*, trans. David A. Dilworth (Tokyo, 1973).

Gayn, Mark, 'Drafting the Japanese Constitution,' in *The Japan Reader 2* (New York, 1973).

Guillain, Robert, *I Saw Tokyo Burning: An Eyewitness Narrative from Pearl Harbor to Hiroshima* (New York, 1981).

Hane, Mikiso, *Peasants, Rebels and Outcastes: The Underside of Modern Japan* (New York, 1982).

Hane, Mikiso, *Modern Japan: A Historical Survey*, 2nd edn (Boulder, CO, 1992).

Hane, Mikiso, *Eastern Phoenix: Japan Since 1945* (Boulder, CO, 1996).

Hasegawa, Nyozekan, 'Make ni jojiru,' *Bungei Shunju* (December 1945).

Hunter, Janet, ed., *Concise Dictionary of Modern Japanese History* (Berkeley, 1984).

Ienaga, Saburo, *The Pacific War: World War II and the Japanese, 1931–1945*, trans. Frank Baldwin (New York, 1978).

Irokawa, Daikichi, *The Age of Hirohito: In Search of Modern Japan*, trans. Mikiso Hane and John K. Urda (New York, 1995).

Ito, Hirobumi, *Commentaries on the Constitution of the Empire of Japan*, trans. Miyoji Ito (Tokyo, 1889).

Johnson, Chalmers, *MITI and the Japanese Miracle: the Growth of Industrial Policy, 1925–1975* (Stanford, CA, 1982).

Kobayashi, Tatsuo, 'The London Naval Treaty, 1930,' in James William Morley, ed., *Japan Erupts: The London Naval Conference and the Manchurian Incident, 1928–1932* (New York, 1984).

Kolko, Joyce, and Gabriel Kolko, 'The Dodge Plan,' in *The Japan Reader 2* (New York, 1973).

Kosaka, Masataka, 'The Showa Era (1926–1989),' in Carol Gluck and Stephen R. Graubard, eds, *Showa: the Japan of Hirohito* (New York, 1992).

Large, Stephen S., *Emperor Hirohito and Showa Japan: A Political Biography* (London and New York, 1992).

Livingston, Jon, Joe Moore and Felicia Oldfather, eds, *Postwar Japan: 1945 to the Present* (New York, 1973).

Lu, David, *Sources of Japanese History* (New York, 1975).

MacArthur, Douglas, 'Statement by General MacArthur on Japanese Draft Constitution,' 6 March 1946, in US Department of State, *Occupation of Japan: Policy and Progress*, Publication 2671, Far Eastern Series 17 (Washington, DC, 1946).

Maddox, Robert James, *Weapons for Victory: The Hiroshima Victory Fifty Years Later* (Columbia, MO, 1995).

Marshall, Byron K., *Capitalism and Nationalism in Prewar Japan* (Stanford, CA, 1967).

Morley, James William, ed., *Japan Erupts: The London Naval Conference and the Manchurian Incident, 1928–1932* (New York, 1984).

Morton, W. Scott, *Japan: Its History and Culture*, 3rd edn (New York, 1994).

Nolte, Sharon, *Liberalism in Modern Japan: Ishibashi Tanzan and His Teachers, 1905–1960* (Berkeley, CA, 1987).

Norman, Herbert E., *Japan's Emergence as a Modern State* (New York, 1940).

Patrick, Hugh T., 'The Phoenix Rises from the Ashes: Postwar Japan,' in James B. Crowley, ed., *Modern East Asia: Essays in Interpretation* (New York, 1970).

Pyle, Kenneth B., 'The Advantages of Followership: German Economics and Japanese Bureaucrats, 1890–1925,' *Journal of Japanese Studies*, 1 (Autumn 1974).

Pyle, Kenneth B., *The Making of Modern Japan*, 2nd edn (Lexington, MA, 1996).

Reischauer, Edwin O., *The Japanese Today* (Cambridge, MA, 1988).

Richie, Donald, 'The Occupied Arts,' in Mark Sandler, ed., *The Confusion Era: Art and Culture of Japan During the Allied Occupation, 1945–1952* (Washington, DC, 1997).

Schirokauer, Conrad, *A Brief History of Chinese and Japanese Civilizations* (New York, 1978).

Seki, Hirohara, 'The Manchuria Incident, 1931,' trans. Marius B. Jensen, in James William Morley, ed., *Japan Erupts: The London Naval Conference and the Manchurian Incident, 1928–1932* (New York, 1984).

Shibusawa, Keizo, *Japanese Society in the Meiji Era* (Tokyo, 1958).

Shigemitsu, Mamoru, *Japan and Her Destiny: My Struggle for Peace* (New York, 1958).

Shimada, Toshihiko, 'The Extention of Hostilities, 1930–31', in James William Morley, ed., *Japan Erupts: The London Naval Conference and the Manchurian Incident, 1928–1932* (New York, 1984).

Sigal, Leon V., *Fighting to the Finish: The Politics of War Termination in the United States and Japan, 1945* (Ithaca, NY, 1988).

Spence, Jonathan D. *The Search for Modern China* (New York, 1990).

Tiedemann, Arthur E., 'Introduction,' in James William Morley, ed., *Japan Erupts: The London Naval Conference and the Manchurian Incident, 1928–1932* (New York, 1984).

Toland, John, *The Rising Sun: The Decline and Fall of the Japanese Empire, 1936–1945* (New York, 1970).

Tolischus, Otto D., *Tokyo Record* (New York, 1943).

Waswo, Ann, *Modern Japanese Society: 1868–1994* (Oxford, 1996).

Yuki, Aisoka, *Sonri seikatsuki* (Record of Village Life) (Tokyo, 1935).

FURTHER READING

Beasley, W.G., *The Modern History of Japan*, revised edn. (New York, 1973).

Cohen, Jerome B., *Japan's Economy in War and Reconstruction* (Minneapolis, MN, 1959).

Dore, Ronald P., *Land Reform in Japan* (London, 1959).

Dore, Ronald P., *Aspects of Social Change in Modern Japan* (Princeton, NJ, 1967).

Dower, John W., *Empire and Aftermath: Yoshida Shigeru and the Japanese Experience, 1878–1954* (Cambridge, MA, 1979).

Dower, John W., *Japan in War and Peace: Selected Essays* (New York, 1993).

Feis, Herbert, *Japan Subdued: The Atomic Bomb and the End of the War in the Pacific* (Princeton, NJ, 1961).

Feis, Herbert, *The Road to Pearl Harbor*, 2nd edn (New York, 1963).

Gluck, Carol and Stephen R. Graubard, eds, *Showa: The Japan of Hirohito* (New York, 1992).

Halliday, Jon, *A Political History of Japanese Capitalism* (New York, 1975).

Hardacre, Helen, *Shinto and the State, 1869–1988* (Princeton, NJ, 1989).

Henderson, Dan Fenno, ed., *The Constitution of Japan: Its First Twenty Years, 1947–1967* (Seattle, WA 1968).

Ibuse, Masuji, *Black Rain*, trans. John Bester (Tokyo, 1980).

Ike, Nobutaka, ed., *Japan's Decision for War: Records of the 1941 Policy Conferences* (Stanford, CA, 1967).

Inoue, Kyoko, *MacArthur's Japanese Constitution* (Chicago, IL, 1991).

Jansen, Marius B., ed., *Changing Japanese Attitudes Toward Modernization* (Princeton, NJ, 1965).

Jansen, Marius, *Japan and China: From War to Peace, 1894–1972* (Chicago, IL, 1975).

Kawabata, Yasunari, *Snow Country*, trans. Edwin G. Seidensticker (New York, 1958).

Kawahara, Toshiaki, *Hirohito and His Times: A Japanese Perspective* (Tokyo, 1990).

Kawai, Kazuo, *Japan's American Interlude* (Chicago, IL, 1960).

Lu, David, *From the Marco Polo Bridge to Pearl Harbor* (Washington, DC, 1961).

Maruyama, Masao, *Thought and Behaviour in Modern Japanese Politics* (London, 1963).

Minear, Richard H, *Victor's Justice: The Tokyo War Crimes Trial* (Princeton, NJ, 1971).

Minear, Richard H., ed. and trans., *Hiroshima: Three Witnesses* (Princeton, NJ, 1990).

Morley, James William, ed., *Dilemmas of Growth in Prewar Japan* (Princeton, NJ, 1971).

Natsume, Soseki, *Kokoro*, trans. Edwin McClellan (Chicago, IL, 1967).

Ogata, Sadako, *Defiance in Manchuria:The Making of Japanese Foreign Policy, 1931–32* (Berkeley, CA, 1964).

Patrick, Hugh, ed., *Japanese Industrialization and Its Social Consequences* (Berkeley, CA, 1976).

Patrick, Hugh and Henry Rosovsky, eds, *Asia's New Giant: How the Japanese Economy Works* (Washington, DC, 1976).

Reischauer, Edwin O. and Marius B. Jansen, *The Japanese Today* (Cambridge, MA, 1995).

Schaller, Michael, *The American Occupation of Japan* (London, 1985).

Shillony, Ben-Ami, *Revolt in Japan: The Young Officers and the February 26, 1936 Incident* (Princeton, NJ, 1973).

Shively, Donald H., *Tradition and Modernization in Japanese Culture* (Princeton, NJ, 1971).

Sievers, Sharon, *Flowers in the Salt: The Beginning of Feminine Consciousness in Modern Japan* (Stanford, CA, 1983).

Silberman, Bernard S. and H.D. Harootunian, eds, *Japan in Crisis* (Princeton, NJ, 1974).

Tanizaki, Junichiro, *The Makioka Sisters*, trans. Edwin G. Seidensticker (New York, 1957).

Tsurumi, Kazuko, *Social Change and the Individual: Japan Before and After Defeat in World War II* (Princeton, NJ, 1970).

Ward, Robert, *Democratizing Japan: The Allied Occupation* (Honolulu, HI, 1987).

Weinstein, Martin E., *Japan's Postwar Defense Policy, 1947–1968* (New York, 1971).

Wohlstetter, Roberta, *Pearl Harbor: Warning and Decision* (Stanford, CA, 1962).

Yoshida, Shigeru, *The Yoshida Memoirs*, trans. Kenichi Yoshida (Boston, 1962).

SEMINAR STUDIES IN HISTORY

General Editors: Clive Emsley & Gordon Martel

The series was founded by Patrick Richardson in 1966. Between 1980 and 1996 Roger Lockyer edited the series before handing over to Clive Emsley (Professor of History at the Open University) and Gordon Martel (Professor of International History at the University of Northern British Columbia, Canada and Senior Research Fellow at De Montfort University).

MEDIEVAL ENGLAND

The Pre-Reformation Church in England 1400–1530 (Second edition)
Christopher Harper-Bill   0 582 28989 0

Lancastrians and Yorkists: The Wars of the Roses
David R Cook   0 582 35384 X

TUDOR ENGLAND

Henry VII (Third edition)
Roger Lockyer & Andrew Thrush   0 582 20912 9

Henry VIII (Second edition)
M D Palmer   0 582 35437 4

Tudor Rebellions (Fourth edition)
Anthony Fletcher & Diarmaid MacCulloch   0 582 28990 4

The Reign of Mary I (Second edition)
Robert Tittler   0 582 06107 5

Early Tudor Parliaments 1485–1558
Michael A R Graves   0 582 03497 3

The English Reformation 1530–1570
W J Sheils   0 582 35398 X

Elizabethan Parliaments 1559–1601 (Second edition)
Michael A R Graves   0 582 29196 8

England and Europe 1485–1603 (Second edition)
Susan Doran   0 582 28991 2

The Church of England 1570–1640
Andrew Foster   0 582 35574 5

STUART BRITAIN

Social Change and Continuity: England 1550–1750 (Second edition)
Barry Coward   0 582 29442 8

James I (Second edition)
S J Houston   0 582 20911 0

The English Civil War 1640–1649
Martyn Bennett   0 582 35392 0

Charles I, 1625–1640
Brian Quintrell   0 582 00354 7

The English Republic 1649–1660 (Second edition)
Toby Barnard   0 582 08003 7

Radical Puritans in England 1550–1660
R J Acheson   0 582 35515 X

The Restoration and the England of Charles II (Second edition)
John Miller   0 582 29223 9

The Glorious Revolution (Second edition)
John Miller   0 582 29222 0

EARLY MODERN EUROPE

The Renaissance (Second edition)
Alison Brown   0 582 30781 3

The Emperor Charles V
Martyn Rady   0 582 35475 7

French Renaissance Monarchy: Francis I and Henry II (Second edition)
Robert Knecht   0 582 28707 3

The Protestant Reformation in Europe
Andrew Johnston   0 582 07020 1

The French Wars of Religion 1559–1598 (Second edition)
Robert Knecht   0 582 28533 X

Phillip II
Geoffrey Woodward   0 582 07232 8

The Thirty Years' War
Peter Limm   0 582 35373 4

Louis XIV
Peter Campbell   0 582 01770 X

Spain in the Seventeenth Century
Graham Darby   0 582 07234 4

Peter the Great
William Marshall   0 582 00355 5

EUROPE 1789–1918

Britain and the French Revolution
Clive Emsley   0 582 36961 4

Revolution and Terror in France 1789–1795 (Second edition)
D G Wright   0 582 00379 2

Napoleon and Europe
D G Wright   0 582 35457 9

Nineteenth-Century Russia: Opposition to Autocracy
Derek Offord   0 582 35767 5

The Constitutional Monarchy in France 1814–48
Pamela Pilbeam   0 582 31210 8

The 1848 Revolutions (Second edition)
Peter Jones   0 582 06106 7

The Italian Risorgimento
M Clark   0 582 00353 9

Bismark & Germany 1862–1890 (Second edition)
D G Williamson   0 582 29321 9

Imperial Germany 1890–1918
Ian Porter, Ian Armour and Roger Lockyer   0 582 03496 5

The Dissolution of the Austro-Hungarian Empire 1867–1918 (Second edition)
John W Mason   0 582 29466 5

Second Empire and Commune: France 1848–1871 (Second edition)
William H C Smith   0 582 28705 7

France 1870–1914 (Second edition)
Robert Gildea   0 582 29221 2

The Scramble for Africa (Second edition)
M E Chamberlain   0 582 36881 2

Late Imperial Russia 1890–1917
John F Hutchinson   0 582 32721 0

The First World War
Stuart Robson   0 582 31556 5

EUROPE SINCE 1918

The Russian Revolution (Second edition)
Anthony Wood   0 582 35559 1

Lenin's Revolution: Russia, 1917–1921
David Marples   0 582 31917 X

Stalin and Stalinism (Second edition)
Martin McCauley   0 582 27658 6

The Weimar Republic (Second edition)
John Hiden   0 582 28706 5

The Inter-War Crisis 1919–1939
Richard Overy   0 582 35379 3

Fascism and the Right in Europe, 1919–1945
Martin Blinkhorn   0 582 07021 X

Spain's Civil War (Second edition)
Harry Browne   0 582 28988 2

The Third Reich (Second edition)
D G Williamson   0 582 20914 5

The Origins of the Second World War (Second edition)
R J Overy   0 582 29085 6

The Second World War in Europe
Paul MacKenzie   0 582 32692 3

Anti-Semitism before the Holocaust
Albert S Lindemann   0 582 36964 9

The Holocaust: The Third Reich and the Jews
David Engel   0 582 32720 2

Germany from Defeat to Partition, 1945–1963
D G Williamson   0 582 29218 2

Britain and Europe since 1945
Alex May   0 582 30778 3

Eastern Europe 1945–1969: From Stalinism to Stagnation
Ben Fowkes   0 582 32693 1

Eastern Europe since 1970
Bülent Gökay   0 582 32858 6

The Khrushchev Era, 1953–1964
Martin McCauley   0 582 27776 0

NINETEENTH-CENTURY BRITAIN

Britain before the Reform Acts: Politics and Society 1815–1832
Eric J Evans   0 582 00265 6

Parliamentary Reform in Britain c. 1770–1918
Eric J Evans   0 582 29467 3

Democracy and Reform 1815–1885
D G Wright   0 582 31400 3

Poverty and Poor Law Reform in Nineteenth-Century Britain, 1834–1914:
From Chadwick to Booth
David Englander   0 582 31554 9

The Birth of Industrial Britain: Economic Change, 1750–1850
Kenneth Morgan   0 582 29833 4

Chartism (Third edition)
Edward Royle   0 582 29080 5

Peel and the Conservative Party 1830–1850
Paul Adelman   0 582 35557 5

Gladstone, Disraeli and later Victorian Politics (Third edition)
Paul Adelman   0 582 29322 7

Britain and Ireland: From Home Rule to Independence
Jeremy Smith   0 582 30193 9

TWENTIETH-CENTURY BRITAIN

The Rise of the Labour Party 1880–1945 (Third edition)
Paul Adelman   0 582 29210 7

The Conservative Party and British Politics 1902–1951
Stuart Ball   0 582 08002 9

The Decline of the Liberal Party 1910–1931 (Second edition)
Paul Adelman   0 582 27733 7

The British Women's Suffrage Campaign 1866–1928
Harold L Smith   0 582 29811 3

War & Society in Britain 1899–1948
Rex Pope   0 582 03531 7

The British Economy since 1914: A Study in Decline?
Rex Pope   0 582 30194 7

Unemployment in Britain between the Wars
Stephen Constantine   0 582 35232 0

The Attlee Governments 1945–1951
Kevin Jefferys   0 582 06105 9

The Conservative Governments 1951–1964
Andrew Boxer   0 582 20913 7

Britain under Thatcher
Anthony Seldon and Daniel Collings   0 582 31714 2

INTERNATIONAL HISTORY

The Eastern Question 1774–1923 (Second edition)
A L Macfie   0 582 29195 X

The Origins of the First World War (Second edition)
Gordon Martel   0 582 28697 2

The United States and the First World War
Jennifer D Keene   0 582 35620 2

Anti-Semitism before the Holocaust
Albert S Lindemann   0 582 36964 9

The Origins of the Cold War, 1941–1949 (Second edition)
Martin McCauley   0 582 27659 4

Russia, America and the Cold War, 1949–1991
Martin McCauley   0 582 27936 4

The Arab–Israeli Conflict
Kirsten E Schulze   0 582 31646 4

The United Nations since 1945: Peacekeeping and the Cold War
Norrie MacQueen   0 582 35673 3

Decolonisation: The British Experience since 1945
Nicholas J White   0 582 29087 2

The Origins of the Vietnam War
Fredrik Logevall   0 582 31918 8

The Vietnam War
Mitchell Hall   0 582 32859 4

WORLD HISTORY

China in Transformation 1900–1949
Colin Mackerras   0 582 31209 4

Japan Faces the World, 1925–1952
Mary L Hanneman   0 582 36898 7

Japan in Transformation, 1952–2000
Jeff Kingston   0 582 41875 5

US HISTORY

American Abolitionists
Stanley Harrold   0 582 35738 1

The American Civil War, 1861–1865
Reid Mitchell   0 582 31973 0

America in the Progressive Era, 1890–1914
Lewis L Gould   0 582 35671 7

The United States and the First World War
Jennifer D Keene   0 582 35620 2

The Truman Years, 1945–1953
Mark S Byrnes   0 582 32904 3

The Origins of the Vietnam War
Fredrik Logevall   0 582 31918 8

The Vietnam War
Mitchell Hall   0 582 32859 4